THE MAKING
INSPECTOR
MORSE

Mark Sanderson has been a committed fan of Inspector Morse ever since the first episode, 'The Dead of Jericho', was broadcast on 6 January 1987. He has been a copywriter for publishers Jonathan Cape, the books editor of *I-D* magazine and reviewer of film and television for *Time Out* magazine. As a freelance writer he has contributed to *The Times*, the *Times Literary Supplement*, *Daily Telegraph*, *Daily Mirror*, the *Independent*, the *Independent On Sunday*, *Radio Times* and *GQ*. Nowadays he is an occasional TV previewer for the *Sunday Times* and is a consultant of the independent TV production company Panoptic which produced both his *Alternative Queen's Speech*, featuring Quentin Crisp, and the talk show series *Out of Order* for Channel 4. The author is thirty-two and lives in Islington, north London, where he is still completing his first thriller.

THE MAKING OF
INSPECTOR
MORSE

Mark Sanderson

MACMILLAN

First published 1991 by Macmillan London

This edition published 1995 by Pan Books
an imprint of Macmillan General Books
25 Eccleston Place, London SW1W 9NF
and Basingstoke

Associated companies throughout the world

ISBN 0 330 34418 8

1 3 5 7 9 8 6 4 2

A CIP catalogue record for this book is available
from the British Library

Typeset by Rowland Phototypesetting Limited,
Bury St Edmunds

Printed and bound in Great Britain by
BPC Paulton Books Limited

To Drew

CONTENTS

FOREWORD

It is now four years since *The Making of Inspector Morse* was published. The fact that it was a progress report rather than the last word on the subject had always been a source of dissatisfaction thus I was delighted to be asked to bring the book up to date, to discuss the sixth and seventh series in detail and record the remarkable grip the series has continued to exert on the British public. Of course the news that Inspector Morse had completed his sabbatical and was returning to the fray was even more exciting. It has not been the same without him. Let us hope 'The Way Through the Woods' turns out to be the first of many more.

INTRODUCTION

Coded messages, murder . . . right up my street. It's not a bad way to start the day

A T 8 p.m. on Tuesday 6 January 1987 ITV viewers saw a gleaming burgundy Jaguar 2.4, registration number 248 RPA, being driven on to the forecourt of a garage. The man behind the wheel was Chief Inspector Morse and this was his first outing on television. In physical terms he was not destined to go very far – seconds later a gang of crooks smashed into the side of his cherished car – but in broadcasting terms the Oxford detective was going to run and run. As a series *Inspector Morse* has proved to be a smash hit.

Today 750 million people around the world tune in to follow the cases of the grumpy, middle-aged policeman. Angolans and Americans, Australians and Zambians, Barbadians and Italians – along with the inhabitants of another forty countries – have all grown to love Morse and his side-kick Lewis, characters created by Colin Dexter and brought to life by John Thaw and Kevin Whately.

'Have you seen the latest viewing figures?' A welcome break in the shooting of 'The Last Enemy'.

A man alone: Morse in typical mournful mode.

Why so many viewers should be prepared to spend a couple of hours in the company of a lonely bachelor, a man whose main pleasures in life are classical music, crossword puzzles and real ale, is one of the questions that this book aims to answer. Others include how the series started, how an episode is made, how the programme has developed through five series and what the sixth holds in store.

Wherever possible the individuals involved – the actors, writers, producers and directors – speak for themselves. The result is an illustrated, behind-the-scenes history of a remarkable success story. Other detective dramas – *Van der Valk, The Ruth Rendell Mysteries* and *Taggart* among them – have attempted, less successfully, to repeat the winning formula of *Inspector Morse*. So far twenty episodes have been broadcast; in Chapter Nine I choose what I consider to be three of the best.

First, though, we travel to Oxford, the home of Morse and his creator, Colin Dexter.

Opposite *Grave thoughts:*
Morse and Chief Superintendent Strange face up to the possibility of an inquiry into the case of the Abingdon Four.

CHAPTER ONE

COLIN DEXTER

There's a lot of story-writers who live in Oxford
'THE SILENT WORLD OF NICHOLAS QUINN'

READERS of the Inspector Morse novels – whether they live in Scandinavia, Japan, Iceland or Brazil – would probably not be surprised to find a book entitled *The Melancholy Man* (a study of Charles Dickens) on the shelves of Colin Dexter. However, they may be surprised to discover that the creator of Morse is a happily married man and father of two.

The despondent detective made his début in *Last Bus to Woodstock* in 1975 but Dexter, who became a teacher after graduating from Cambridge in 1953, had written three books before that. 'They were intended to show students how to get into Oxbridge,' says Dexter. 'Two of them were on General Studies and the third was on politics, which I wrote with a friend. When you're asked what you think of freedom or democracy you need to be on nodding terms with great men like Marx and Hegel. The idea was that if you read these books you'd be able to tackle a little more easily such questions as "What is happiness?"'

Morse might never have been born if the sun always shone in North Wales. 'In 1972 I was on holiday and it was raining – it's not unknown, is it? – and when the children had finished complaining I hadn't much to do. I had a tedious day ahead. I'd read all the books that were there and thought I might be able to write a crime novel as good as the lousy one I'd just finished, so I sat down and wrote the first chapter of *Last Bus to Woodstock*. It wasn't more than four or five pages but the holiday finished and I forgot all about it. Six months later I went back to it and thought the material seemed much better than it had at the time of writing – so I carried on. I used to write in the evenings, after listening to *The Archers* and before going out for a pint of beer. If you only write a page a night that's 365 pages a year or one and a half books.

'I'd been told that it was a good idea to have three publishers in mind. I sent the typescript to Collins first. They kept it a very long time. After almost six months it was returned to me with a wonderful letter of six pages – one of the best criticisms I've ever had – saying it was good but not good enough to pass muster. If you listen to criticism too much you'll never do anything so I didn't change a word and sent the typescript to number two on the list,

Opposite Actor and creator: John Thaw and Colin Dexter on location during 'The Silent World of Nicholas Quinn'.

Macmillan. George Hardinge, Lord Hardinge of Penshurst, who was then in charge of the crime list, was in bed with flu at the time but within forty-eight hours he rang me up and asked me to come and see him. So I went to London. "Look," he said. "I'm going to do your book. It's clearly a first novel, you've got some things to learn, but I don't want you to change a thing." That's the difference between two publishers. There's a lot of luck in it.'

A Scottish journalist chose *Last Bus to Woodstock* as his book of the year. 'It wasn't extensively or rapturously reviewed,' recalls Dexter, 'but crime writers in this country don't receive much attention unless they're well known. The local press were good to me – I used to compile crosswords for them. I re-read it recently in preparation for an omnibus edition and thought it wasn't bad, although it reads a bit like a travel book in places. I remember Edmund Crispin [a crime writer (1921–78) whose own detective, Gervase Fen, is a professor of English Literature at Oxford] wrote to George Hardinge and quoted me as saying that on one particular page something was done with "commendable promptitude" when what I meant was "quickly". I could have changed it for the new edition but I didn't think that would be right.'

Dexter came to Oxford in 1966 to work for the University Examination Board. 'I went very deaf in school-teaching and couldn't quite cope.' He retired due to ill-health in 1988 but still works for the Board on a part-time basis each summer: 'I've never been a full-time writer.' Since Dexter is a Latin and Greek scholar it is easy to see where Morse gets his interest in the classics. The character was named after Sir Jeremy Morse, the chairman of Lloyds Bank; Morse is an old Oxford name and Sir Jeremy an inveterate crossword solver. But where did Morse come from in the first place?

'He was rather like Athena who sprang from the head of Zeus, fully grown and fully blown,' says Dexter. 'He hasn't altered in my mind at all, not two hoots. I wanted him to be very clever, I've always enjoyed people who can do crosswords in two minutes. They have a cerebral quickness and the ability to come to an immediate conclusion – even if it's the wrong one – without hesitation. I always liked John Dickson Carr's fictional detectives, Gideon Fell and Sir Henry Merrivale, because of this. They were both based on Chesterton and wore black cloaks and shovel-hats.

'Morse is a semi-autobiographical character, he shares my passion for Wagner, crosswords, beer and women. Even if you change your character traits, the attitudes expressed are determined by what you are. If you think about society, politics or religion, whatever you write is going to be a personal reaction. On the other hand Morse can be mean-minded, mean-spirited and mean-pocketed, and I think one of the great crimes is to be reluctant to pay your round. I would put that above adultery. Morse is

sometimes unimaginative in the way that he reprimands someone in front of their colleagues. That's a terrible thing to do. I would never do that. I'm a placid sort of person.

'I knew what I was doing from the word go. I think Morse is melancholy rather than morose. He has a quiet humour. He's aware that the world has gone slightly sour which, of course, it has. You only have to look at the news to see that we are staggering from crisis to crisis. He knows that everything is not as it should be. He is pessimistic about the way we are running the planet and so am I.'

Every Inspector Morse novel has been written in Dexter's first-floor study which overlooks a splendid garden. 'I write in longhand. I write in biro. The first draft is very rough. I just go through the story from A to B. That's the hard work. Then I write it all out again in a more orderly and ordered form. Finally I go through it once more, give it a bit of tarting up, then send it off to be typed by someone else.' The quotations that precede each chapter in most of the books are added after the writing but before the typing. 'I'm fortunate in knowing quite a bit about literature – not the prose writers but the poets. I don't find it difficult. It's just a harmless bit of self-indulgence.

'I get quite a few ideas from being deaf,' says Dexter, 'because I mishear so much.' The obvious example would be *The Silent World of Nicholas Quinn*, first published in 1977 and dedicated

Crossword puzzled: Morse without a clue in 'Service of all the Dead'.

Bar-room philosophy: Morse and Lewis water their brains in 'The Dead of Jericho'.

to Jack Ashley. 'I knew exactly what was going to happen from the very nature of the book. The sleight of hand has to begin immediately. A fundamental deception takes place because one name is gone for instead of the other, i.e. Doctor Bartlett rather than Donald Martin.' Quinn, who wears a hearing aid, makes a mistake lip-reading at a drinks party.

'In the same way the first chapters of *The Dead of Jericho, Service of all the Dead* and *The Wench is Dead* were all determined by their last chapters. The first relies on a series of pronoun changes, the second on a phoney church service and so on. But I don't always know whodunnit. With *Last Seen Wearing* it is possible for half a dozen characters to have done the deed till ten pages from the

end. I knew who I wanted to have done it but some people accuse
me for not having gone for the juiciest candidate.'

Once he has an idea the legwork begins. 'I never do anything
without an enormous amount of topographical research in Oxford.'
To mark Dexter's acute sense of place a Morse Trail has been set
up in and around the city, avoiding the main tourist attractions in
favour of lesser-known spots such as Holywell Cemetery. 'The
cemetery is only five minutes from Radcliffe Square,' says Dexter,
'but it's wonderfully quiet and semi-unkempt. There are several
famous bodies there.

'I was perfectly well aware that if I had any strengths in writing
they would be in plotting and mise-en-scène rather than anything

*Phoney murder: Morse at
home during 'Service of
all the Dead'.*

In stitches: Max sees that Morse gets the needle in 'The Silent World of Nicholas Quinn'.

to do with police procedure. I know nothing about the police and that's a very good thing if you're going to write whodunnits because if you get a murder here you're not going to get Morse and Lewis walking up to the front door. Most crime is localised, rather crude, uninteresting and certainly not cleverly devised. A man walks into the police station with a dagger dripping with blood saying, "I'm sorry but I've knifed the missus." This is what life is about. Most detectives have several cases on the go at once and spend most of the time taking statements and rooting through files which is hardly gripping stuff. The only adviser I had was a friend down the road who was a pathologist. Before he died I would ask him, for instance, what a corpse would look like if it had been in the canal for three weeks. He would say, "It could be green or blue or black but certainly not white."'

Writing involves another kind of legwork too. 'The Romans had this motto,' says Dexter, '"*solvitur ambulando*", which roughly translates as "walk about to work it out". Once you start writing ideas begin to happen in an almost physical way. The Brontës used to walk around the table muttering all kinds of incantations. In each chapter you set off to find something out, for example, where the corpse has spent the previous two nights. It's amazing when you put it down on paper how things turn out slightly differently from what you thought. If you sit passively and just wait for something to happen you're unlikely to write very much. It's much better to bash ahead.'

It is this sense of getting somewhere, of making progress, that keeps the reader turning the pages and the viewer glued to the box. 'There has to be a sense of development,' says Dexter. 'Story-lines, whether in books or on TV, are very important. People like stories

*Fishy circumstances:
Colin Dexter (right) as an
extra in 'The Last
Enemy'.*

*A prayer for the dying:
Ruth Rawlinson at the
'Service of all the Dead'.*

– that's why Homer, Virgil and Ovid were so popular. I'm sure if they were alive today they'd be writing for TV.

'If Kenny McBain hadn't read my books Morse would never have been on television. That is the only reason, there was no hype at all. He rang me up out of the blue and said, "I know your books. I like them. There's a possibility of Central funding a series. I'd like to come and see you." So he came to Oxford with the writers, Anthony Minghella and Julian Mitchell, and we went down to the pub and had a meal. We talked about the music of Janáček of all things.'

So far all but three of Dexter's nine novels – *The Riddle of the Third Mile*, *The Secret of Annexe 3* and *The Wench is Dead* – have been adapted for television. For his ninth, Dexter took the story-line he had devised for writer Julian Mitchell – 'The Wolvercote Tongue' – and developed it in such a way that it would have been imposs-ible to film. The result was a completely different whodunnit.

'Kenny said, "We've got to change certain things",' says Dexter. 'Well, if you're going to be televised you say yes to every-thing. You say, I'll give *you* some money if you like.' Most of the changes have been cosmetic. For instance, Morse's Lancia became a Jaguar. Plots have been streamlined and minor characters dropped to fit the two-hour format. Morse's lustfulness and depen-dence on alcohol have been toned down, and the seedier locales of Oxford generally eschewed to widen the appeal of the pro-gramme. But the Dexter hallmarks of intricate plotting, humorous reproach and weary world-view have survived intact and provide the bedrock of the series' success.

The biggest change has been in the character of Lewis. In the novels Lewis is a contemporary of Morse, a rather dull, not to say dim, man with a Welsh wife and grown-up children. Despite all the other differences, however, the TV Lewis has inherited his love of chips. 'I think they were sensible to want a much younger Lewis,' says Dexter. 'The surrogate father/son relationship works very well. The differentiated accents, as opposed to two vaguely southern ones, are more interesting too. People tell me that they can't help but hear John and Kevin when they read the books now, but when I'm writing I don't consciously think of John at all even though I think he is a fine performer and one of the main reasons for the continued success of the series. My view of Lewis has changed though. I've solved the problem by ignoring it and not giving him too much physical description.'

Dexter's novels contain much besides straight narrative: scraps of letters, time-tables, diary entries, gravestone inscriptions, news-paper extracts and crossword clues. Two favourite clues – with the same solution – that aren't included in the books are 'Person with crimes to unravel' (Dexter's own work) and 'Tec with no Mrs – so

ripe for entanglement' (by R. J. Hooper, a fellow solver). The answer isn't far away. Although the screen version of *The Silent World of Nicholas Quinn* retains the vital acrostic, most of these word-based clues are lost on TV. However, photographs, pictures and videos have proved to be neat visual equivalents that are used in a similarly playful way. 'Last Seen Wearing', 'Who Killed Harry Field?', 'Greeks Bearing Gifts' and 'Promised Land' all feature videos in which crucial information can be glimpsed. It is in the same spirit that Dexter makes a fleeting personal appearance in nearly every film.

'Kenny thought it would be a nice little tribute to me as the author if I were to appear in the first film,' says Dexter. 'After that it became a bit of a joke. I always go along and spend a day on the set if I can. Everyone is very kind. I've known some of them for a long time now. I usually like to be a by-stander or a by-sitter in a pub because, whereas you can fiddle red or white wine and Scotch, you can't fiddle real ale.

'Television is a medium in which you can't be sure of anything. So many people have an input that you can never be certain how anything is going to turn out. The first and second series were based on my novels then I wrote the plots for the third series. That was fifty or sixty or seventy pages in five months. I told Kenny afterwards that I could never do it again because it would send

Tea-break: Thaw and Whately take time out during the filming of 'The Silent World of Nicholas Quinn'.

me mad. Nowadays they send me the scripts and I make a few suggestions. I occasionally write a bit of dialogue otherwise I just keep an eye on Morse. You've got to have someone keeping an eye on the characterisation, his vocabulary and attitudes. I'm a kind of consultant.'

Dexter believes that as a crime writer there are three main accolades. 'The first is to be mentioned in *Private Eye* and that has happened to me several times. The second is to be awarded a Dagger by the Crime Writers' Association.' *Service of all the Dead* and *The Dead of Jericho* received Silver Daggers. *The Wench is Dead* was awarded the Gold Dagger for the best crime novel of 1989. 'The third is to have a book included in the summer selection that the Royal family take to Balmoral each year.' Last summer *The Jewel that was Ours* brightened up at least one Scottish holiday. 'I think Princess Margaret is a fan.'

'I've been very lucky,' the father of Inspector Morse modestly concludes. 'The television series has made me better known – I'm always being asked to give talks and interviews. I receive hundreds of letters. You should feel gratified that people know who you are. I think the nicest thing is to feel that you have written a good book and be told so. Nowadays I get singled out a bit more but apart from that it hasn't made any difference. I still mow the lawn and do the washing up. The trouble is I don't get much time for writing.'

Fear not, the tenth Inspector Morse novel is on its way. 'I might call it *The Final Analysis*. You may remember some time ago *The Times* reported the strange case of a man who gave the police a sort of chess problem that supposedly led to the spot where a body was buried. This gave me the idea for the book. I wrote a few chapters some months ago and it's time I went back to it. I'm sure Morse will make a hell of a mess of it.'

Forced to name the best crime writer of all time, Dexter plumps for Agatha Christie. 'Five or six of her books are in the top ten. She had by far the most fertile imagination in terms of plot twists. Above all she gives the reader a big, fat, troublesome mystery.'

The same can be said of Dexter.

Opposite *A couple of characters: Colin Dexter and John Thaw.*

PROD INSPECTOR MORSE III — THE GHOST IN THE MACHINE

DIRECTOR : HERBIE WISE | CAMERAMAN : MICHAEL DAVIS

SLATE 347 TAKE 1

24TH AUG 1988 DAY ~ INTERIOR

CHAPTER TWO

IN THE BEGINNING

Background information can always be useful
'THE SILENT WORLD OF NICHOLAS QUINN'

I N matters of detective fiction Agatha Christie is never far away. She is also partly – if indirectly – responsible for the birth of *Inspector Morse*.

'It all started six years ago,' says Ted Childs, Central Television's Controller of Drama and Executive Producer of the programme from day one. 'I was impressed by the fact that there was then a series of Agatha Christie adaptations being transmitted by the BBC starring Joan Hickson as Miss Marple. They had been written by people like Alan Plater [author of *The Beiderbecke Affair*] and were doing quite well. I thought it was something that Central ought to be into.' It should never be forgotten that independent television companies are in the business of making money. More often than not, entertainment or art are just fortunate by-products. With *Inspector Morse*, however, the art of film-making and the art of making money became one.

'I mentioned this in passing to Kenny McBain, who was then producing the first series of *Boon*, and he said, "I've been reading these novels by Colin Dexter. They feature a detective and they're set in Oxford." The fact that they were set in our own TV region was useful so I read the books – I've still got them somewhere, it was summer so they're stained with Ambre Solaire – and we pondered about it. Kenny went off and talked to Colin Dexter and there was some toing and froing after that. Eventually I approached our then Director of Programmes, Andy Allan, told him I thought this was a good idea that should be pursued and that Kenny should be commissioned to develop it.'

They got the green light. It was at this stage that several decisions were taken, key decisions that were to play a major part in the success of the series. 'Kenny and I both felt that we ought to pitch it up a bit in the sense that we should try and get the best writers we could interested and available to work on the project. Kenny knew Anthony Minghella and approached Julian Mitchell. It was about this time that Kenny convinced me that the show ought to be two hours rather than one, which was something of a departure. The original novels are quite complex and, having talked to the writers, we were certain that, creatively speaking, the

Opposite Morse code: the clapperboard used on the shoot of 'Ghost in the Machine'.

adaptations would be more effective in a two-hour cycle rather than one. In TV terms, allowing for commercial breaks, this means one hundred and four minutes rather than fifty-two.'

Such a proposal was not welcomed by all the TV executives involved. 'A lot of people were reluctant to endorse this innovation,' says Childs. 'The belief was that an ITV audience would not sit and watch a rather convoluted piece of fairly intense detection for two hours. Andy Allan was a bit surprised at first but he was very supportive and responded positively to the arguments that we put to him. Kenny and I believed that you can go wrong by talking down to your audience so we decided to make three films and see what happened. We felt that if they were well crafted, well written, well acted and well directed they would work.'

As the producer of *The Sweeney* Childs had got to know John Thaw very well. 'I thought John would be good in the role of Morse as the writers and Kenny were beginning to conceive of him. I thought it about time he had another drama series so John, Kenny and I met to talk about it. We gave John some material to read and, quite properly, he wanted to think it through. He asked a lot of questions but in the end he was persuaded that we thought he could do it and that he would enjoy doing it.'

That left the part of Sergeant Lewis.

'The classic problem in adapting detective novels is that the detective has to talk to someone so that he can let the viewer know how he is proceeding with his investigations, making his deductions and surmising. Kenny thought Kevin Whately would be good in the role of Lewis and I agreed. I had worked with Kevin on *Auf Wiedersehen Pet* which Witzend Productions had made for Central in our studios at Nottingham.'

Inspector Morse was never envisaged as anything but a collection of films – it would not have been the same as an ordinary TV series – but this immediately meant it would cost more. 'We always knew that it would be a relatively expensive show,' says Childs, smiling wryly. 'We initially planned to make it at our Birmingham studios but we didn't have enough film capacity to service this kind of production because we thought it important to make as much of it as possible in its original setting. Consequently it was agreed that Zenith, which at that time was owned by Central, would make it for us, although we retained creative control over it and Kenny was the producer.' Zenith, who have since made such programmes as *The Paradise Club* and *Chimera*, is now jointly owned by Carlton Communications and Paramount.

The price of the first series came to something like £3 million, that is £1 million per film or £500,000 per screen hour. Today, over five years later, that has risen to £600,000 per hour. 'The first series

Chorus of disapproval: Morse fails to see the joke in 'The Dead of Jericho'.

was well received – not overwhelmingly well received – but it did sufficiently well on its first outing to justify making a second series,' says Childs. 'This time we made four films. After that it clearly took off and became a great success. It had the singular advantage in commercial terms of delivering a large audience which contained demographically within it a high socio-economic quotient. In other words we were getting people who had money watching it and who would buy the things that the advertisers were trying to sell. Recently advertisers have been very keen to criticise the ITV system for not providing a BBC 1 type audience. It's the difference between *The Times* and the *Sun*, if you like. It's comparatively rare to appeal to both kinds of readers at the same time. *Inspector Morse* does this. It is a jewel in our crown.'

Even so, without foreign sales the programme would make a loss. 'Our budget is rather more than the price we get for it from the ITV network. That said, it is one of the few shows that has managed to achieve a second peak-time showing on ITV and a third/first showing on Channel Four. It seems to have a very attractive durability and has sold widely round the world. The bean-counters keep telling me, though, that you have to take into account the cost of currency and distribution expenses, but in terms of cash return there's no doubt that it has done well.'

After the first two series McBain felt that he needed a change

Burning the midnight oil: Morse doing his homework in 'Deceived by Flight'.

and went off to work on *Sharpe*, a Napoleonic drama set in Spain, which, for various reasons, was never made. Chris Burt, who had also worked on *The Sweeney*, was brought in as the producer of the third series before going on to develop *The Free Frenchman* and *The Woman in Black*. Kenny McBain planned to return to produce the fourth series but, after an eighteen-month battle with Hodgkin's disease, he died on 22 April 1989, a few days after *Inspector Morse* received a Queen's Award for Export. It was a tragic loss. However, his brilliant brain-child was to go from strength to strength.

'Kenny was one of my closest friends,' says Anthony Minghella, who wrote the script of the first episode, 'The Dead of Jericho'. 'In 1981 I gave up my job as a university teacher to become a writer. I planned to move down to London but before I could do so I got a call from the BBC asking me if I would like to work for them as a script-writer. Having just given up a full-time job, I was reluctant to accept but they told me to come over and have a meeting. I travelled down from Hull and Kenny picked me up from the station. He said, "I'm the producer," and I asked, "What's the programme?" His reply was, "*Grange Hill.*"

'He was a very articulate, sensitive, belligerent man. He was a strange combination of the rough Glaswegian – he laid his Scotch accent on with a trowel – and an excellent pianist who had studied at Harvard. His complexity is reflected in what he saw in the

Men of Morse: Kenny McBain and Colin Dexter.

Inspector Morse books. He knew that it was possible to have a mainstream drama series about a single man who liked classical music.'

Minghella went on to write the episodes entitled 'Deceived by Flight' and 'Driven to Distraction'. In the latter Morse reminisces about a friend who, although terminally ill, was concerned that the battery of his car would go flat. It is a touching moment made all the more poignant because it is based on a true story. 'Just before Kenny found out he was dying,' recalls Minghella, 'he had bought a very nice Saab. He got worried about it just standing outside and the battery going flat. So I would go round and drive the car for him. It was a curious thing, driving it all round north London and taking it right back to where I'd started . . . What upsets me is that he never lived to see just how successful *Inspector Morse* turned out to be.'

CHAPTER THREE

'THE DEAD OF JERICHO'

I'm quite a different kettle of fish, Lewis
'The Dead of Jericho'

NOBODY had ever seen anything like it. The date chosen to launch *Inspector Morse* was auspicious: 6 January is Twelfth Night, the Feast of the Epiphany. 'It was an epiphany that people had an appetite for a whole evening's viewing, that not everybody is impatient and keeps switching channels,' says Anthony Minghella who was born on 6 January. 'It is very difficult to make TV into an event but *Morse* forces you to settle down and devote two whole hours to it.'

From the very beginning 'The Dead of Jericho' demands your attention. The startling title sequence, which immediately establishes the mix of high-brow and low-brow that is one of the main characteristics of the series, intercuts a choir practice in the chapel of an Oxford college with a falling-out among thieves. The soundtrack, courtesy of Barrington Pheloung, splices William Byrd with Mozart and rock. It is a Saturday morning. Morse has decided to take his car into the garage on his way to the rehearsal, but arrives just as the rumpus breaks out. In the heat of the moment he handcuffs a young mechanic to the handle of his car door although this does not stop him pulling away when he sees that some of the crooks are about to make a spectacular getaway. He is not quick enough – they smash into the side of his beloved Jaguar. It needs more than a paint job now.

Delayed by the incident, Morse – a true singing detective – at last takes his place in the front row of the choir but only in time for the final two bars. Laughter breaks out and Morse looks sheepish. Rueful humour proved to be one of the hallmarks of the programme. Indeed 'The Dead of Jericho' contains all the features that the later films went on to develop. Within minutes we are told that Morse does not use his first name. Accused of being silly, he replies, 'It was my parents who were silly.'

The plot, based on the novel by Colin Dexter, centres on the suspicious suicide of Anne Stavely, a fellow chorister whom Morse has been awkwardly wooing. It is a typically complicated story, involving a pair of brothers, a peeping Tom, adultery, blackmail and a gay drug addict who blinds himself. When Morse finds a copy of *Oedipus Rex* by the victim's bedside he is convinced that

Opposite *Singing detective: Morse in full voice.*

Opposite *Pregnant pause: Anne Stavely faces the truth.*

'the man who killed Anne Stavely is called Sophocles'. 'Who's he when he's at home?' asks Lewis. This is the first instance of Morse's desire that life should imitate art. In this case it doesn't, but, as we shall see in Chapter Nine, three years later in 'Masonic Mysteries' he is not at all happy when his wish is finally granted.

Minghella chose to adapt 'The Dead of Jericho' out of all of Dexter's novels because it was the one that he liked the most. 'It had a real sense of place and is very wintry, dark and oppressive but, as it turned out, we had to film it in summer. Because I'd written quite a few night scenes most of them had to be dropped.' Even so, the one in which Morse turns up at Canal Reach to discover it blocked with police vehicles, blue lights flashing in the black, underlines how right McBain was to insist on location shooting with film. It is wonderfully atmospheric. The title sequence was his idea too. Given that the episode is a modern Greek tragedy – if not a reworking of the Oedipal myth – it seems only right that it was called the *proagon*.

'In times of classical Greek drama,' explains Minghella, 'the actors would go round the villages in advance of the plays and perform a trailer – not the highlights but certain characteristics, enough to make you want to see the play when it came round the following week. We wanted you to stay put for two hours.' It worked and, as the series has developed, the writers have exploited the breaks to the full, switching locations, jumping in time and thus setting up and encapsulating the mystery that Morse and Lewis will eventually solve.

Besides establishing most of Morse's character traits – his love of cars, crosswords, booze, music and women – the first episode also lays the foundations of his relationship with Lewis. When Chief Superintendent Strange informs Morse that he is not going to be promoted he tells him, 'You're a clever sod but you don't say the right things to the right people. You never will.' Morse is very rude to Lewis. Rude and patronising. 'Are you ragging me?' demands Lewis when Morse is discussing Sophocles. He is riled. 'At least I can survive half an hour's work without reaching for a beer glass.' 'That's a good idea,' says Morse. It is Lewis's birthday but he still ends up buying the beer and, to add insult to injury, he is shocked by the price of real ale. 'Happy birthday,' offers Morse at last.

'I thought it vital to introduce Lewis as soon as possible into the series,' says Minghella. 'There's something very stupid about Lewis in the books but I thought it important that Lewis be shrewder than Morse and more generous as well. He is partly in awe of his superior and his labyrinthine thought processes. Lewis is a complete man, Morse is incomplete, fragile.

'In "The Dead of Jericho" Morse is much less sure of himself

Birthday boy: Lewis getting on in 'The Dead of Jericho'.

than he becomes later. The writing is very fractured. Morse and Anne Stavely can hardly say a word to each other. I saw him as someone who was socially inept. The fact that more than one person writes for the series is one of its strengths. I think it just as well that Julian Mitchell wrote the other two episodes in the first series, he brought style to it. He's epigrammatic. Everybody used to say that whereas Julian finishes all his sentences, I couldn't finish any of mine.'

Stereo man: Alan Richards, maker of excellent hi-fis, with his lookalike brother Anthony.

It is only when Lewis says 'we haven't met' to Anthony Richards, and so reveals that his brother Alan has been impersonating him, that Morse finally solves the case. The tradition of Lewis making an innocent remark that provides the key to the mystery was to continue until at least the fourth series.

Certainly the plot is ingenious and exciting, with numerous suspects, but the most remarkable aspect of the opening film is the way in which its style and tone have remained intact ever since. This is a tribute to how much the series had been thought out in the first place.

Director Alastair Reid keeps the camera moving so that the action flows from scene to scene. He fills the episode with menace and exploits the possibilities of film to the full, using a variety of lenses to give depth and scope. For instance, when the blackmailer George Jackson (Patrick Troughton, the second Dr Who) lies in wait for Alan Richards to dump the money in a waste-bin beside a telephone box at the crossroads, a wide-angle lens and long shot emphasise the isolated nature of the spot. The camera is positioned in such a way that the roads cross in the centre of the frame, the red call-box standing out in contrast to the surrounding green grass. After he has retrieved the cash and is pedalling home, the character is shot from a very low angle which has such a foreshortening effect that it appears that the car behind him will surely run him over.

The attention to detail – Anne *Stavely* is a music teacher,

Messing about on the river: a beautifully atmospheric establishing shot from 'The Secret of Bay 5B'.

Jackson is said to have been repointing a wall in her back garden, the wall of Jericho? – and the care with which the action is lit have been maintained throughout each series. When so much television seems ill-considered and slapdash the sheer quality of the opening programme is attractive. The haze in the chapel; the sun streaming into the gloomy court-house; the dazzling, antiseptic, white light that silhouettes the blind boy in hospital; and the soft blue of dusk help to create a pervasive sense of melancholy. After all, as far as the audience is concerned, this is Morse's first lost love and his first taste of death.

Colin Dexter makes his first appearance in 'The Dead of Jericho' too. When Morse is on his way to visit Ned Murdoch in college towards the end of Part Two, Dexter, wearing a light jacket, walks past him in the arcade. For a few moments he and John Thaw are the only people in view.

The episode ends as it began, with a cruel joke. Lewis, eager to prevent Anthony Richards escaping, drives Morse's newly repaired Jag into the path of the car. Morse's pride and joy is smashed in exactly the same place as before.

Minghella has also experienced fearful symmetry. 'I was in New York. I don't know if you do this but the first thing I do when I get into a hotel room is to turn on the television. I did so, the screen flickered and there were the words "written by Anthony Minghella". It was *Inspector Morse*. It was like a gag, a strange joke. It was the weirdest thing. It was "The Dead of Jericho".'

Barrington Pheloung, composer of the theme music, is one of the few people to have worked on every single episode of *Inspector Morse*. He is also responsible for all the other music that is heard in each film. He became involved with the series after Anthony Minghella took Kenny McBain to see his play *Two Planks and a Passion* for which Pheloung had provided the music.

'The brief was to compose a theme that represented a very complex character,' says Pheloung, 'the most essential feature being that Morse is a chronic melancholic who fails in his relationships with women. It also had to represent a great romantic, a man who had studied the classics, a man who loves classical music and a man who likes crosswords. He isn't that different to me really.

'The fun side of the work was the cryptic element. I found a table of Morse code and spelled out Morse's name. The dots and dashes fit nice and snugly into a rhythmic counterpoint which is a leitmotif that has played in the series for over five years now. It starts off on a sine wave played on an electronic keyboard and then is picked up by the violins. With that came a harmonic structure and then the tune just wrote itself. The Morse code insinuates triple time, a sense of three. Against that you have the tune that is in duplets, which means you have two against three, and then the quadruplets come in so you have four against two against three plus plenty of hemiolas. It's actually very complicated for a signature tune but it was always meant to be a germ for thematic and symphonic development, music for the cinema rather than TV.'

Although Pheloung comes from Sydney his surname is Huguenot. He is an excellent mimic and can turn into John Thaw or Kevin Whately at will. The following words on Kenny McBain are delivered in thick Glaswegian.

'Kenny became a very dear friend of mine but because of this he was a pain in the bum to work for. He was very demanding. When I took him the first demo tape he said, "It's a bit too modal, Baz – it needs to be more Brahmsian," so I went away and wrote this very Brahmsian piece which took a very long time. He thought it was wonderful but he had one complaint – it was too Brahmsian. I was in a no-win situation so I went back and delicately remixed the original idea. This time it was "perfect". That was Kenny for you.'

Besides composing all the original music for the series – nine sixties rhythm and blues tracks for 'Who Killed Harry Field?', four Australian country and western numbers for 'Promised Land' – including 'Keep On Truckin' Till You're Dead' and 'Eighteen Wheels of Love Heading for Your Front Door' – Pheloung orchestrates all the classical music that we hear on the programme. It is more cost-effective to re-record works than pay for the use of particular recordings.

*Music man: Barrington
Pheloung on location in
Italy.*

'It all started when Kenny was rueing the fact that he couldn't
find a cheap recording of a Beethoven quintet,' says Pheloung. 'I
said that's ridiculous, four of the people in our band played the
piece last week, let us do it. The music is played by a group of
session musicians who happen to be the best in the world, all of
whom are members of leading string quartets or chamber orches-
tras. Whatever I give them to play, they invariably nail it in one
take. I studied and went to college with most of them and now I
conduct them. That's my other job in real life, I'm a clippie.'

Technology has speeded up the laborious process of arranging
the scores. It took a week to orchestrate the music for 'The Dead
of Jericho'. Today the musical soundtrack for each episode can be

Not a pretty picture: Morse holds up one of Harry Field's artworks after someone has thrown acid over it. The missing part of the picture is a vital clue to who killed him.

completed in one day. 'I love painstakingly reconstructing exact versions,' confesses Pheloung. 'That's the strength of modern musical notation, you can reproduce every tiny nuance of phrasing.' In 'Driven to Distraction' he recreates two Ella Fitzgerald songs, 'You Do Something To Me' and 'Why Can't You Behave?', and in 'Who Killed Harry Field?' the Fats Waller classic 'Ain't Misbehavin'', fluffed notes and all. 'I had letters from real buffs asking me which recording I'd used,' says the composer with glee.

*A peck from Pickford:
Morse on the receiving
end of Emma's attentions
in 'Fat Chance'.*

'When the series is running I get around two hundred letters a
week.'

There's no doubt that the music of *Inspector Morse* is popular.
Last year, the album reached number four in the charts and gave
Pheloung his first platinum disc. A second album is in the works.
A celebratory concert at the Royal Festival Hall on 25 May 1991
was a virtual sell-out. This is a tribute to the cunning choice of
classical pieces. Wagner apart, if Morse had a passion for

An audience of one:
Morse listening to
Randal Rees in the
Oxford Union.

Shostakovich, Webern or Stockhausen it might well be a different story. You can't go wrong with Puccini, Bach, Beethoven, Schubert and Mozart.

Pheloung's fondness for crosswords is reflected in the way he plays games with the listener just as some directors play games with the viewer. In 'The Last Enemy' an interview with a top civil servant is conducted to the sound of the strings of a samisen being plucked. Thus an oriental instrument provides the perfect accompaniment for a Whitehall mandarin. Innocent passers-by can be implicated by a sudden chord-shift or a clue to whodunnit suggested by subtle use of Morse code. In 'Who Killed Harry Field?', for example, Pheloung spells out the culprit's name – Eirl – all over the orchestra.

One of the most satisfying moments for Pheloung comes in 'Fat Chance' where there is a suggestion that Morse may have actually spent the night with Emma Pickford. When he enters the police station the next morning there is certainly a spring in his step and a smile on his face. This momentous occasion is signalled by the theme music which is heard in a major key for the first time in five years – in other words in C sharp. 'These are the kinds of things that you can have fun with,' says Pheloung. 'The music is far more about Morse as a man than anything else. I hate violence. I hate death. I don't want to sensationalise it. I try to convey the suspense and horror of it rather than the excitement and the adrenal rush.'

Although Pheloung plays a large part in each film and can be heard on many of the soundtracks – thanks to multi-tracking, he and a friend are able to create the effect of a whole choir – he only physically appears in one. He is the first person to be seen in 'Masonic Mysteries'. However, it is impossible to tell that it is him because he is Papageno and inside a giant bird's head.

'We recorded a third of *The Magic Flute* in one three-hour session for that episode,' says Pheloung. 'It is an extraordinary piece, the world's best opera, the world's best musical, there's a hit song every two minutes. Colin Dexter laments that we have weaned Morse off Wagner but if Morse is a true lover of classical music he'd have to return to Mozart. Mozart, clearly and patently, towers above all other composers. It's him you can listen to at 4 a.m. when you've just finished working. Time and again I've said I'll just listen to that trio and ended up listening to the whole opera.

'It's the most mental thing in the world to write music for a living,' concludes Pheloung. 'You have to write so much to pay the mortgage.' He has written over one hundred film and TV scores, *Boon* and *Portrait of a Marriage* among them. In the past ten years he has composed forty-seven ballet scores. In the past twelve months he has written twenty-eight hours of music. 'I wrote ninety-six minutes of music last week, that's more than Mozart ever did in seven days.' In spite of all this Morse is especially important to him. 'The thing is you can't help but love the old bugger.'

CHAPTER FOUR

JOHN THAW

He's one of the good guys, Morse
'FAT CHANCE'

'I WAS doing a Ray Cooney farce, *Two Into One*, in Toronto with Daniel Massey – and getting pretty fed up with it – when I was offered the part of Morse,' says John Thaw. Three years later Thaw, as the Chief Inspector, and Massey, as Anthony Donn, met again as old friends in 'Deceived by Flight'. Donn gets done in and Morse gets whodunnit.

'I wouldn't have accepted the role if Morse had been remotely like Regan,' continues Thaw, lighting up. 'The fact that he was so different to Steely Jack was an attraction.'

At the age of twenty-one Thaw was already understudying Sir Laurence Olivier in a West End play called *Semi-Detached*. He took over from him twice, once for a whole week. At the age of twenty-three he was starring in his own television series, *Redcap*, but it was as another detective that he really made his mark. The fifty-three episodes of *The Sweeney*, broadcast between 1975 and 1978, made Jack Regan and John Thaw household names.

On the surface there is certainly little similarity between Regan and Morse apart from the fact that they are both policemen. Underneath, though, they have a lot in common. Both are characters in ground-breaking drama series, both are unconventional detectives, both have little success with women and both come into conflict with their superiors. 'I do that. I rub people up the wrong way,' admits Morse in 'Driven to Distraction'. Both are disillusioned men who still show courage in pursuit of convictions. They both reflect the emotional toll that the job imposes. Morse is a grown-up Regan who thinks first and acts later. He uses his brain rather than his brawn. The violence is restricted to a lashing of the tongue. And one of the many strengths of Thaw as an actor is his ability to convey rage and frustration without resorting to histrionics or ham.

Although fans of *Inspector Morse* may be aware of the diversity of his roles on television, they may not know that Thaw is an equally accomplished stage performer. The man who played a crime reporter for LWT in *Mitch*, the long-suffering father in *Home to Roost* for Thames and Stanley in Kingsley Amis's *Stanley and the Women* for Central is the same man who played Toby Belch in *Twelfth Night* and Wolsey in *Henry VIII* for the Royal Shakespeare Company. Other theatre roles have included Nick, the barman in William Saroyan's *The Time of Your Life*, and Dick Wagner, the Australian journalist in Tom Stoppard's *Night and Day*. It was no

Opposite *Trouble brewing: Mrs Radford weeps after finding her dead lover in a tun at the family brewery.*

small achievement for the sixteen-year-old son of a Mancunian lorry driver to get into the Royal Academy of Dramatic Art. It was an even greater achievement to win the Vanbrugh Award for his portrayal of Mephistophiles while he was there and the Liverpool Playhouse Award, ensuring him a year's work in rep as soon as he left RADA. Thaw has always tried to maintain a balance between theatre and TV throughout his career. He still hopes to tackle *King Lear* for the Royal Exchange Theatre in Manchester.

When he accepted the role of Morse Thaw was forty-four. He is not at all troubled that he has now reached his half-century because, as he has said on more than one occasion, 'I was born looking fifty.' The important point is that his crumpled, lived-in face is perfect for the mournful copper. Does he share any of his characteristics?

'I'm more akin to Morse than Regan but that's not saying much. I'm not a crossword buff, it's all I can do to finish the *Evening Standard* crossword. I haven't got that type of brain. I don't like beer. I never have liked beer. I hate it. When we're filming we use low-alcohol beer. I have tried real ale, the proper stuff, and can see what people go on about but I've given up drink now anyway. In terms of music, though, Morse likes what I like.'

When he appeared on BBC Radio 4's *Desert Island Discs* in 1990 Thaw chose works by Bach, Sibelius, Puccini, Elgar, Schubert, Mozart and Richard Strauss. Only Sibelius and his fifth choice – 'Little Girls' from *Annie*, sung by his wife Sheila Hancock – have not been featured in *Inspector Morse*. The book he elected to take with him was *The Wind in the Willows*.

'I hadn't picked up any detective fiction since I'd read Sherlock Holmes at school,' recalls Thaw. 'I have to confess that at the time I'd never heard of Colin Dexter. My reading tends towards non-fiction. I enjoy his books now and read them for total relaxation. Like Kenny McBain and Ted Childs, I thought they contained something that we could build on.'

Indeed it is fascinating to see how Morse has changed over the years. To begin with, in terms of what he wears, he has smartened up his act. In the first series the detective's good taste does not stretch to his wardrobe. In 'The Silent World of Nicholas Quinn' Morse sports a blue shirt, a red tie and a waistcoat. In 'The Dead of Jericho' he clearly sees nothing wrong with wearing a green shirt with a grey tie. When he breaks into Anne Stavely's house he dons a leather coat and a trilby.

'The feeling was that he should be a tasteless dresser because clothes are the last thing on his mind,' says Thaw. 'He's the kind of man who makes one trip a year to Burton's or Austin Reed and that's it. He would buy six or seven shirts at one go. After the first series it was felt that we had gone too far that way. After all, he is

a Chief Inspector and there would be certain people he would have to meet. Besides, even he – living in his own little world – would agree that it would not be right to conduct interviews in a red polo-neck and a green jacket.'

The third series has him in white shirts, brown suits and a terylene bathrobe, but in the fourth and fifth Morse appears positively dapper in several sharp outfits that would not look out of place in Next. Lewis in his double-breasted suit could pass for a yuppy. However, it has now been decided that the duo were beginning to look like any pair of policemen in London. Dark suits are fine in the Met but Oxford is provincial, tweeds and cords predominate, so a return to duller mix-and-match jackets and ties is on the way.

Whether Morse's wardrobe can be held partly responsible for his lack of success with women is difficult to ascertain. Every one of the early films finds Morse falling for a damsel in distress. Ruth Rawlinson sobs in his arms in 'Service of all the Dead'; Sheila Williams cries her heart out while embracing him in 'The Wolvercote Tongue'. For the first two years he doesn't get anywhere. 'I've never had any feelings for you,' says Jane Robson in 'The Settling of the Sun'. The viewer finds it hard not to hate her. She turns out to be a baddy anyway.

'The job gets in the way, maybe. I get in the way. Maybe I'm

Head shots: the headmaster's wife learns whodunnit in 'Last Seen Wearing'.

Face to face: Grayling and Morse dance a quickstep in 'The Secret of Bay 5B'.

the job,' muses Morse in 'The Secret of Bay 5B'. Quizzed on the subject by a high-class whore in the same episode, he suggests that he is 'too choosy, too hesitant, too lazy [and] too busy.' There was an element of crowd-pleasing in the prolonged flirtation of Morse and Grayling, the curvaceous pathologist, in the third series which left the detective, for once, in a happy mood. In the fourth Emma Pickford's kiss in 'Fat Chance' got the tabloids fizzing. So heaven knows what they'll make of Morse french-kissing an opera singer in 'The Death of the Self', one of the forthcoming films in series six.

The end of the affair: Dr Kemp and Sheila Williams in the Randolph Hotel.

Opposite *Deadly diva: Frances Barber in 'The Death of the Self'.*

Opposite *Blind fury: car salesman Boynton watches Morse watching him in 'Driven to Distraction'.*

One of the reasons why millions of people have grown to love the detective is that he is unmistakably human. We see him with all his faults. The question of his libido is not ignored. When Morse and Lewis visit the girls' school in 'Last Seen Wearing' Morse asks his sergeant, 'Have you ever thought about the person who designed the sports skirt? Somebody sat down, drew a fantasy and made it compulsory uniform. I can never watch Wimbledon without thinking of that man.' A danger of this warts-and-all approach is that Morse could be seen as just a dirty old man. Thaw avoids this by treating Morse's lust with a gentle humour. 'They say sex can be very good for the over sixty-fives,' says Morse in 'The Wolvercote Tongue'. 'Oh, do they?' replies Lewis. Morse goes on, 'Especially if you didn't get much before sixty-five.'

Cell divisions: DCI Dawson encounters an old adversary (out of shot) for the second time around.

But it is not only in his private life that Morse gets things wrong: his *modus operandi* leaves something to be desired. Chief Inspector Dawson in 'Second Time Around' describes him as 'a poor policeman and a very good detective'. 'I sometimes – *sometimes* – get things arse about face,' admits Morse in 'The Secret World of Nicholas Quinn'. His method relies on inspiration rather than application, and occasionally this leads to conflict with the dogged Lewis. Morse's hounding of Boynton regardless of lack of

'Too much sang-froid all round': Lady Hanbury in 'Ghost in the Machine'.

evidence provokes this outburst from him in 'Driven to Distraction': 'There's no procedure. It's crime solved like a crossword puzzle and I'm sick of it.' 'I stumble around, that's what I do,' says Morse in 'Deceived by Flight'. That's why we like him. It wouldn't be easy to like someone who was always right, who, like some misplaced Mountie, always gets his man.

Morse is bloody-minded: 'As soon as somebody doesn't want to discuss something, I do' ('Service of all the Dead'). He is embarrassed both by his first name – 'Everyone just calls me Morse' could be his catchphrase – *and* his nickname, Pagan ('Deceived by Flight'). He is pedantic: 'You'll never get on if you can't master your subjunctives, Lewis' ('Ghost in the Machine'). He suffers from vertigo. Stomach churning, head swimming, at the top of St Oswald's in 'Service of all the Dead', he shouts at Lewis, 'I'm scared of bloody heights, you stupid sod.' His dependence on booze – 'There's always time for another pint' ('The Silent World of Nicholas Quinn') – has been played down but his reliance on his Jag – 'I can't think in these other cars' ('The Dead of Jericho') – and music – 'I can't think without music' ('Driven to Distraction') – are touching. The best episodes, and Thaw's best performances, are those which show Morse at his most vulnerable. Having nearly been stabbed by his instructor in 'Driven to Distraction', Morse mumbles, 'It sounds stupid but I can't get my hands off the wheel.' There is a terrific moment in 'Masonic Mysteries' when Morse, wrapped in a red blanket in the back of an ambulance, cries, 'Where's Lewis? I want Lewis.'

'I think after twenty films Morse is not as hard on Lewis, he is more tolerant,' says Thaw. 'They are more relaxed together but the lines are still drawn. Morse is still the master and he still treats Lewis like a servant sometimes.' This is made absolutely clear in

Opposite Getting the point: nasty driving instructor Derek Whitaker reaches the end of the road in 'Driven to Distraction'.

Being taken for a ride:
Lewis in 'The Last
Enemy'.

'The Sins of the Fathers' when the hapless sidekick arrives at Morse's flat to find him changing a tyre on his car. Morse immediately goes in to wash his hands: 'Put that wheel on, Lewis.'

'When we get to the scenes with Lewis it's almost like coming home,' continues Thaw. 'Morse obviously trusts Lewis totally and Lewis has great respect for Morse as a policeman. In the same way there's a trust between Kevin and I as actors. It's very important, that feeling of trust. It's good that it comes over.'

Thaw learns his lines the night before. 'When we started the first series I used to learn four or five days ahead but it was so mentally tiring it was silly. It got to the point where I was sitting up till two in the morning trying to cram it in as you would for a stage play. For the last two or three years I've gone home, washed and changed, then looked at the next day's script. It's the first thing I do. On average it takes an hour or an hour and a half. If you have big speeches then it obviously takes longer. Rightly or wrongly, I believe it's better to do it while Morse is fresh in my mind. Only then do I have something to eat.

'It's not getting harder – to be honest it's always been hard – and it's certainly not getting any easier. New writers have new styles. The next film, ''Absolute Conviction'', is by John Brown, a writer new to the series, so I know before I start that it will be harder to learn than Alma Cullen's or Julian Mitchell's stuff. You get used to their styles. You can almost – and I say almost – guess what the next line or word will be.'

Ironically, one of Thaw's greatest skills is to let the viewer know what he is thinking and feeling without saying a word. How does he do it?

'By thinking it! It's as simple as that. There's a scene in an episode of the new series, "Dead on Time", which requires Morse to go from shock and surprise to grief and then to anger, real anger, in about thirty or forty-five seconds and, dare I say, I did it pretty well. I haven't seen it but they tell me that it works. I felt every thought. I actually went through that range, those three things, in that space of time. That's all it is. That's the actor's job. If you think it and believe it the audience will too.'

Does he use his own memory and personal experiences to create the emotion?

'No I don't. Morse is always encountering corpses but I've never seen anybody dead. I don't know what it's like, I just imagine it. Then I am being Morse, Morse reacting to that. It's not John Thaw. John Thaw might well react totally differently to finding a dead body. He might throw himself on it, rush out of the room or run round the block, I don't know. Morse can't run out because he has lines to say! After the scene I've just described I was shaking. It does have that effect on you and yet it has to be like flicking a switch because you might have to do it six times. Every time, though, you have to be able to do it one hundred per cent, to recreate that genuine emotion. When you flick the switch you have to know what the machine can do.'

Is it depressing playing a depressive? He waves a hand at the crew. 'These scallywags won't let me get depressed. Morse is saddened by what he has to deal with. He doesn't know anything else. He sees the awful side of people all the time. The downside of humanity is his life. That's why a lot of people watch, they are intrigued by this slightly overweight, white-haired little man. They are interested in the way this rather eccentric policeman goes about his business.'

Which are his favourite episodes?

'I bore people with this but Kenny always used to say we're making films not a "series". Any episode should be able to stand up on its own. Even if you've never even heard of Morse you should be able to watch one and enjoy it as a single piece of work. I think the three that do this particularly well are "The Dead of Jericho" which was the first one we ever did, "Promised Land" because I relished the chance to extend the character and "Masonic Mysteries" which also pushed Morse a little further.'

In September 1991 the National Film Theatre in London screened a season of John Thaw's work. *Inspector Morse* was rep-

Bodywork: Dr Russell getting down to business in 'The Last Enemy'.

resented by 'The Dead of Jericho'. After more than twenty films it would be all too easy for Thaw to free-wheel, just to go through the motions, but he has striven to continue developing his character. In March 1990 Thaw received the BAFTA award for Best Television Actor. He deserved it.

'It is difficult to remain fresh,' says Thaw. 'The longer a programme continues the harder that gets. Once shooting starts you're on a treadmill. You have to find new ways of approaching it. When you start you're instinctively looking for that all the time. If I ever get the feeling "sod it, I know how this scene goes" I'll stop. I packed in *The Sweeney* because I became bored with it. Of course, when I left Regan behind I did feel bereft. You feel affection for all the parts you play, even if it's only a small one in rep for three weeks. No doubt I'll feel the same about Morse.

'I've always done *Inspector Morse* on the basis that if I'm enjoying it when I'm asked to do another series then I'll do another one. So far I'm enjoying making the sixth series and I have been asked to do another. But I'll tell you this. If – *if* – I do another series next year, that will be it, definitely. The seventh series will be the last.'

When the sad day comes, and the script is being written for the final episode, would he allow Morse to be killed off?

'I know Julian Mitchell would be champing at the bit to do it.

It has been his ambition for three years. He had this wonderful fantasy. An opera singer is involved in a murder and Morse travels to Germany to solve the case. He gets everything right and is getting nearer and nearer to the truth. His instinct is spot on. One evening he goes to Bayreuth to see Wagner's *Götterdämmerung* and a terrorist leaves a bomb in the bar. Morse dies through no fault of his own but he dies all the same. Anyway, the idea was knocked on the head. Julian still says he's the only man allowed to kill off Morse, but I think Colin Dexter would have something to say about that. So would I. No pun intended, but it would be over my dead body.'

CHAPTER FIVE

KEVIN WHATELY

There aren't too many like Lewis
'WHO KILLED HARRY FIELD?'

COINCIDENTALLY Kevin Whately was in a similar position to John Thaw when Morse was first mentioned. 'I was in a play directed by Ray Cooney when they approached me to play Lewis,' says Whately. 'I'd met Kenny McBain in Nottingham while I was doing *Auf Wiedersehen Pet* and he was producing *Boon*. The fact that our series got higher ratings than his riled him a bit and there used to be this joshing rivalry between us. Kenny obviously thought that I'd be a good foil for John so I went along and read with him. Fortunately the play that I was in did not transfer to London and doubly fortunately they kept the part of Lewis open for me.

'When I saw the first script I loved it straightaway. I could see the quality of Anthony Minghella's writing – it jumped off the page. I didn't really know John when we began because I was starting in rep – working every night – when *The Sweeney* went out and so I saw very little of it. Even so I knew we were doing something that was going to be good.'

Whately served his theatrical time – 'I played everything really' – in Perth, Stoke-on-Trent, Newcastle, Worcester and the Old Vic in London. By the end of the seventies he was touring the country with left-wing theatre groups such as 7:84. 'I was doing bits of television as well but TV seemed to take over as the eighties started.'

His first part on television was in a drama-documentary for the BBC about the race to develop the miner's lamp between Sir Humphrey Davy and George Stephenson. He appeared in the medicated soap *Angels* and even did a six-week stint in *Coronation Street*. 'I played a lorry driver called Kevin who was dating Elsie Tanner's assistant in the caff. This girl kept going away on overnights with the lad so when he dropped her back late for work the next day there'd inevitably be a terrible fracas with Pat Phoenix.' However, it was a stage play, *Accounts* by Michael Wilcox (who later wrote 'Last Bus to Woodstock' for *Inspector Morse*), that led to *Auf Wiedersehen Pet*.

'The play was first produced at the Traverse Theatre in Edinburgh,' says Whately. 'It was so successful that it transferred to

Opposite Sticky wicket: Lewis going out to bat as a porter of Lonsdale College in 'Deceived by Flight'.

the Riverside Studios in London. It won several awards. We did it for the radio as well. It was a good time – my future wife was in the cast too – and the piece got me noticed. It was turned into one of the first films made by Channel Four but I was too old to play the elder brother by then.

'I wasn't too happy about going from playing a Geordie in one series to playing a Geordie in another but Kenny twisted my arm until I couldn't refuse – "You do Lewis as a Geordie or you can't do him at all!" I did the accent as mild as I could so it was like Brian Redhead's. To begin with I was afraid that Lewis was going to be a turnip-head. At the time there was a series on the BBC, a fly-on-the-wall documentary about the Reading police, which showed the cops crime-busting and drug-busting. They called themselves "turnip-heads". Lewis is not stupid. He's definitely a plodder but he's none the worse for that.'

It is the contrast between Morse and Lewis that creates the dramatic conflict. 'I think Lewis is ahead of Morse in the life-stakes,' says Whately. 'He has his life sorted out even if he hasn't thought it out, that's to say, worked out who he is and what he wants out of life. He's more adept at coping with the everyday world but Morse is ahead of him in terms of brain-power. Morse is inspirational whereas Lewis finds things out by very slow deduction and donkey work. Morse thinks laterally, takes huge leaps in the imagination then finds out if his solution is possible. Lewis has more common sense.'

Time and again, it is Lewis who provides the method for Morse's madness. His habit of thinking out loud often leads Morse to the correct conclusion – even if it is by way of a chance remark: 'See you in the morning' ('Last Bus to Woodstock'); 'Well, she can drive' ('Ghost in the Machine'); 'You reckon she'll stay with him when the money runs out?' ('The Sins of the Fathers'). 'You've done it again, Lewis,' acknowledges Morse in 'The Silent World of Nicholas Quinn'.

Given that Lewis is such an invaluable help and that over the years his boss has come to rely on him more and more, he still has a lot to put up with. In 'Last Seen Wearing', from the second series, Lewis, much to Morse's annoyance, asks to be dropped off at a supermarket because his wife has told him to do the shopping. Morse waits for him outside and is rewarded with four cans of bitter. Instead of thanking his generous sergeant, Morse pronounces the gift 'undrinkable' and hands it back. This ungraciousness is partly caused by Morse's virtual inability to express anything other than dislike and depression. Affection makes him uncomfortable.

'Morse has always been rude to Lewis but it's slightly more balanced now. You can see that Lewis is aware that Morse needs

Getting to grips with a problem in 'The Silent World of Nicholas Quinn'.

him, that he is grateful at times. On the other hand Lewis has become thicker-skinned. The insults bounce off him. They don't wound him very much.'

It was a wise decision to develop the relationship between Morse and Lewis in the third series but at times they are perhaps *too* friendly. There is too much grinning and not enough grit between them. Elsewhere the prickliness in their relationship prevents it becoming sentimental. 'In the first couple of years I was fighting the buddy-buddy relationship that was all the rage after *The Sweeney* and *The Professionals*,' says Whately. 'I tried to emphasise that Morse and Lewis are of different rank, that it is more a question of master and servant. They also have very distinct, separate life-styles.'

As *Inspector Morse* has progressed, the viewer has been treated to tantalising glimpses of Lewis's family life. It seems as if his relations cover the globe. While his wife's Aunt Cissie lives in Wolvercote, he tells Dr Russell that he has an uncle in Jesmond ('Ghost in the Machine') and, in 'Promised Land', his disappointment at not visiting his kin in Gateshead is alleviated by the fact that he has cousins in New South Wales. No wonder Morse feels lonely.

Lewis plays cricket with his son in 'Deceived by Flight'. Morse, sitting on a swing in the back garden, makes a one-handed catch and actually laughs. In 'Masonic Mysteries', their video pre-set to record *EastEnders*, Lewis takes his wife Val to see *The Magic Flute*, as a favour to Morse. They don't stay long: 'What does he see in it? I still couldn't understand a bloody word. Let's go for a drink.' And, in 'Greeks Bearing Gifts', Val speaks her first words and orders Greek food in the Acropolis taverna. Lewis, of course, has the chicken.

'We discussed the matter of Lewis's family with Kenny at the start,' recalls Whately. 'I thought it would be better if his wife were always "her indoors". It leaves more to the imagination that way. That said, there was this lovely scene in "The Dead of Jericho" where Lewis, who was running Morse home, had to stop off at his own house to call in for something on the way. Because it was Lewis's birthday his family had laid on a surprise party for him and Morse suddenly found himself in the middle of all this cloying domesticity. It was a wonderful scene but it was too long and never even shot.'

Whately attributes Lewis's bashfulness to his being a family man. In 'Last Seen Wearing' Lewis can't bring himself to say 'sex' or 'abortion'. 'You're such a prude, Lewis,' says Morse, amused. 'When you've got small kids at home,' says Whately, 'you end up talking like one. There are certain things you don't say in front of the children.'

Whately, too, is a family man with a daughter aged eight and a son aged six. He, like Lewis, comes from the North East and is clearly a very nice man. 'A very, very, very nice man,' replies the actor, laughing. But how similar is Lewis to the man who portrays him?

'He's probably quite similar to me in a lot of ways. I'm plodding, I don't get flustered easily, there's not a lot that upsets me. I'll give people plenty of chances, I forgive them their foibles. I like faults in people, they don't put me off them. I empathise with Lewis completely but I do that with all my characters – even if they're a mass murderer I try to find where they coincide with me and find some sympathy for them. I don't feel that Lewis is me, though, or that I'm him.'

He is evidently not as literal as Lewis and, as an actor, he is much more culturally aware. There is a delightful moment in 'The Infernal Serpent' when Morse is talking to Mrs Copley-Barnes, a frightfully snobbish Master's wife who only teaches the piano to the most gifted of children. Lewis chimes in, 'I bought my nippers one of them electronic keyboards,' and is met with silence. 'As a matter of fact I have bought my children an electronic keyboard,' says Whately. Would he let Morse be as rude to him as he is to Lewis? 'I probably would, yeah. OK, I'm very like Lewis.'

Whately, in common with John Thaw, learns his lines the

evening before shooting. 'If you're very tired you can sit and stare at them for two or three hours before you realise that nothing's going in. Other times you look at it and you know it's there. Some writers are easier to learn than others. Some writers produce scripts that come off the page well. Others, who I will *not* name, are just impossible.' He laughs. 'I never speak the lines out loud till we come in the next day. It's not a great mystery. I don't make any notes on the script either. I just ring all the 'LEWIS's in pencil. If

you have a big day ahead you're never quite sure if it's there but running through it for camera rehearsals gives you confidence, that it's all in there somewhere. I still occasionally get a crisis of confidence with a particular scene. It can be because you're tired or don't quite believe in what you're doing at the time. You have good days and bad days like anybody else except that, because the camera is right there, it shows up more. You can't escape.

'The scenes between Morse and Lewis are the most straight-forward because we trust each other, we know roughly what the other is going to do. You're not desperately trying to think what your character would be doing because, after five years, it's second nature. The terrible thing about filming, though, is that you're often working with actors who only have two days – it may be the only two days they work that summer – and it is a much bigger deal for them. For John and myself it's just another day at the office but they have to make an impact at once. Often this is what gives a scene its electricity.'

Does he ever get bored when Morse and Lewis sit down in their office to mull over yet another complicated case?

'I don't get bored easily. I have a high boredom-threshold. In the old days we used to film the police station sequences earlier in the schedule and you might be talking about six characters when you had so far only met two of them. It was difficult to keep them in your mind then and remember what they'd been up to. Nowadays we tend to do these scenes towards the end of a shoot.'

Has he understood every single plot?

'No. Most of them. Once or twice over the past five years John and I have sat in the trailer and said, "If he knew that there's no way that could have happened," and talked it round and round in circles for fifteen minutes before realising that if we tried to change a word the whole thing would collapse like a house of cards. We usually come to the conclusion that it's best to just go ahead and say it.'

It can't be easy playing Morse's sounding-board all the time. It says much for Whately's performance that Lewis seems just as fresh-faced and enthusiastic now as he's always done. Like Thaw, Whately is surprisingly modest. 'I'm far more proud of the films and the way they look than of what I've done. It's easier for me. I just have to react. John is the driving force. That's much more difficult to do.' Although Lewis has to play second fiddle he has grown with the series and has gained in importance. So has his following.

'It's changed my life completely,' admits Whately, discussing the success of *Inspector Morse*. 'It means that I can afford to pick and choose what I do in the break. I think it's important to recharge your batteries. For instance last year I was in a play called *Our Own*

Opposite *'Let us hypothesise': Morse and Lewis think on their feet in 'The Last Enemy'.*

Kind at the Bush Theatre in London. I've always liked working in the subsidised sector. The director asked me to play the dad who was a very sympathetic, plodding and diligent man. When I read the part my heart sank but in the middle of the play there was a ghastly National Front supporter who delivers this huge political diatribe. I really fancied doing that. When the director asked me if I liked the play I said I thought it was wonderful and his face lit up – but it fell when I said I'd rather play the baddy instead of the dad. An hour later he phoned me up to say I'd got the part.

'There aren't many good sides to being famous. People do love the series. You don't have anybody coming up and swinging a punch at you because you were horrible to your wife on telly the night before. There was something about *Auf Wiedersehen Pet* that was like being part of a rock group. Fans would come up to you, slap you on the back and say, "Hello, mate, how yer doing?" *Morse* appeals to the middle classes as well and they're a bit more reticent about approaching you. If they do they say, "Thank you, I really enjoy it" and then they're off. They don't really want to bother you. With *Auf Wiedersehen Pet* it was more intrusive. From that point of view *Morse* is better. Perhaps it's because Lewis is a policeman.

'Being approached doesn't bother me any more except when the kids are around. If I'm asked for my autograph when they're with me I find it excruciating because they don't understand the concept of the autograph. I've never understood it so I don't know how they're supposed to. My daughter's just getting to the age when she doesn't like people coming up to me in the street. She gets very clingy. They watch tapes of *Morse* but a schools programme I did to teach children how to read is repeated quite often and that gets them a lot more kudos.

'I remember the week I left drama school,' says Whately. 'I went down to the DHSS to collect my cards or something and Anthony Booth was signing on. *Till Death Us Do Part* had just finished but it was a huge hit at the time. That really brought home to me how precarious success can be.'

Sergeant Lewis is much more than a useful device that allows us to see inside the Chief Inspector's head. Thanks to Whately and the writers he is a fully-fledged character who, by interacting with Morse, enables other aspects of both detectives to come to light. 'I don't think Lewis is indispensable,' says Whately, 'but I'd be really sad if the series went on without me.' So would millions of other people. How many of them could name the sidekicks of Wexford or Taggart?

Inspector Morse has some of its greatest scenes when Morse and Lewis are together on screen. There are many humorous and moving moments that bear this out. Lewis making a catch in the

Keeping an eye on the baby: Lewis prepares to save the day in 'Greeks Bearing Gifts'.

cricket match in 'Deceived by Flight'. Chuffed to death, he looks over to Morse to gauge his reaction. Morse is asleep in a deckchair. It is as if he has let his son down. Morse catching Lewis smiling indulgently at himself and Dr Russell in 'The Last Enemy' – it makes a change for Morse to be patronised rather than to patronise. Morse complaining in 'Ghost in the Machine', 'That's what I hate most about this job, breaking the bad news.' 'I know,' retorts Lewis, 'that's why you always make me do it.' Morse and Lewis doing the washing up in 'Second Time Around'. And, most typically, at the end of 'Greeks Bearing Gifts', where Lewis is literally left holding the baby.

Perhaps the best one of all comes in 'Who Killed Harry Field?' when Morse is upset to discover that Lewis is thinking of applying for promotion and a transfer into the Traffic Division. They are sitting outside a country pub. 'I want to get on,' says Lewis. 'I have to have your recommendation . . . Do you think I'm good enough to be recommended for promotion?' Morse says nothing. Then, very slowly, 'I'm sorry to tell you, Lewis . . . that the answer to that . . . is yes.'

CHAPTER SIX

THE WRITERS

Research, detection, similar trades, really
'LAST SEEN WEARING'

'NOBODY has the faintest idea who writes for television, unless it's Dennis Potter,' says Julian Mitchell, who has so far scripted six episodes of *Inspector Morse*. 'They might know Alan Bleasdale but most people who watch TV have no idea that it is written at all – they think the actors make it up. They really do. Following the "Promised Land" episode one of my neighbours in Wales said to me, "I'm sorry to hear that Kevin Whately won't be in the next series," and I said, "What do you mean? Of course he'll be in the next series." "No, no," she said. "I read it in the *Argus*. You see the one you did when they went to Australia – by the way, I didn't like that one very much, I prefer it when they're in Oxford – after they'd finished he got his wife to go out there because he liked Australia so much and she said let's stay so they did and he's not going to be in the next series. I read it in the *Argus* so it's got to be true."'

It is a tribute to the quality of the writing – and the performances – that viewers have no difficulty in believing that Morse and Lewis are real people and not simply actors delivering lines. In some ways *Inspector Morse* is a very 'written' series, the words carry more weight than in most television programmes. It is the visual equivalent of a good read. 'The Silent World of Nicholas Quinn', for instance, hinges on the fact that, when spoken, Donald Martin and Doctor Bartlett appear to a lip-reader to be virtually the same words. This befits a drama in which the leading character is a lover of crosswords and literature. At the close of 'Service of all the Dead' Morse concludes that the case – which involves two tramps – has shades of Samuel Beckett's 'Waiting for Godot'. Lewis, of course, pronounces the silent 't'.

Mitchell, a burly fifty-six-year-old with an unruly beard and a Santa Claus chuckle, is no stranger to Oxford or the University. He received a first-class degree in history while attending Wadham College and later spent a year doing research at St Antony's College. A novelist, playwright and screenwriter, he is perhaps best known for his award-winning play based on the Guy Burgess story, *Another Country*, which was turned into a film starring Rupert Everett in 1984. When I spoke to him he was – in addition to working on his seventh episode for *Inspector Morse*, 'Cherubim and Seraphim' – busy adapting William Golding's sea trilogy for Yorkshire Television and the latest John le Carré, *The Secret Pilgrim*,

Opposite Best seat in the house: a crane is used to get an overhead shot of the celebrating coppers in 'Second Time Around'.

for the BBC. 'I've just moved house and I've got to pay for it somehow.'

A telephone call started it all. 'I didn't know Kenny McBain and I'd never read Colin Dexter but I was suddenly rung up by my agent saying Kenny wanted to meet me and would I read these detective stories. I was extremely doubtful about it because, to tell you the truth, I gave up reading detective stories when I was about fifteen. Until then I'd read nothing but detective stories, P. G. Wodehouse, Agatha Christie, Biggles and Dornford Yates. After that I went straight on to T. S. Eliot and W. H. Auden and became a frightful high-brow, pompous youth. So I hadn't read a detective story for twenty or thirty years when these arrived and I thought they were rather good, actually, and I particularly liked the character of Morse. I was offered two to write in the first series, "Service of all the Dead" and "The Silent World of Nicholas Quinn" which I still think is the best story Colin ever wrote. I thought they were very clever and lots of fun so I thought why don't I do them? What am I being snobbish about? So we set off. Nobody had any idea it would be so wonderfully successful.'

Like Dexter and Morse, Mitchell also enjoys word games. When, in 'Ghost in the Machine' (which was written by Mitchell and based on an idea by Dexter), Lewis says to Lady Hanbury, 'He does crosswords, Madam, he knows all sorts of words that nobody ever uses,' he could be referring to any of the three men. In Mitchell's 'Masonic Mysteries' Macnutt, 'the fount of all wisdom', is named after D. S. Macnutt who, as Ximenes, compiled the crossword for the *Observer* magazine for many years. Incidentally, his successor, Jonathan Crowther (Azed), provides the name of the Rochester expert in 'Last Bus to Woodstock'. 'Now that I've got back into detective fiction,' says Mitchell, 'I actually think it is a wonderful genre because you can do anything up to a point. It's like some kind of very formal poem – there is a problem that has to be solved and you start at the beginning and know that at the end of two hours it has to be solved. It's like writing a sonnet and, moreover, writing for ITV is similar to writing rhyme schemes because of the ad breaks which break the story up into four acts. It's like writing for the theatre as well because you know there has to be an interval whereas, with the BBC, ninety minutes is a hell of a long time to go without a break. It's all very satisfactory, the symmetry of the thing has its own pleasures that are difficult to explain but they *are* there.'

The use of music in *Inspector Morse* is also important to a writer; like word games it can be used to emphasise and complicate a theme. Morse deduces that Lady Hanbury got the idea for her husband's 'suicide' – Lord Hanbury is supposed to have flung himself from the roof of his country house – from *Tosca* when he remembers that Tosca threw herself off the castle walls in Rome. Sometimes the musical references are not spelled out. 'There are usually a couple of jokes for opera buffs tucked away,' chuckles Mitchell. 'Most people don't get these jokes – they're not meant to – but it doesn't matter. Because the actor knows about them they give a kind of solidity to the whole thing. We all like to play games but they are not important. My favourite joke is in "Masonic Mysteries" when the tape that had the bomb in it was a recording by a particular conductor. We had to be a bit careful. David Lascelles's father, Lord Harewood, runs the English National Opera so we asked him for advice. We had originally chosen Sir George Solti but he was still alive so in the end we plumped for Toscanini!'

Once he is given the go-ahead to write an episode, how does he begin?

'You've got to have an idea. The hardest part of all writing is having the ideas, the writing is relatively simple. The early ones were based on Dexter's books or his ideas and story-lines, little stories and sketches.' The way each script takes shape can be seen from the pages reproduced later in this chapter.

'"The Service of all the Dead" still has the highest body count of any Morse episode. Colin did once say to me, "Of course if there really were that number of psychopaths about in Oxford, there would be nobody left alive at all" but that is just the conventions of the genre. I think the plots have become less preposterous as we've gone on so that they are now more psychologically realistic. The idea for "Masonic Mysteries" [which is based on Mozart's *The Magic Flute*] probably came from the Welsh National Opera, with whom I have connections – that's how I know which operas Morse will have seen at the Apollo Theatre in Oxford, the WNO tours there – and the joke that everybody thinks that all policemen are Masons.' The germ of the idea must have been gestating for a long time. In 'Ghost in the Machine', Mitchell's previous contribution, Morse asks Lewis if he is a Mason. No, he replies, 'I might have been a Chief Inspector if I had.'

'The Australian episode came about because John Thaw wanted us to go abroad somewhere to give the crew a break as they do work frightfully hard. I was writing the Robert Altman film *Van Gogh* at the time and so I did an outline of an episode set in Holland so that I could research both of them at the same time. It was nothing like *Van der Valk*, I avoided Amsterdam and carefully set it in places like Haarlem and Dordrecht but in the end it fell through. When this plan resurfaced later on I'd been talking to one of the series' police advisers and the idea came up of the supergrass and how you send someone away. The whole idea of the supergrass is that he is a man with a secret. Who knows that secret? Is it a true secret or a false secret? I got interested in that and then

Beer buddies: Lewis and an Australian colleague get drunk together in 'Promised Land'.

we decided to go to Australia because that is one of the countries where supergrasses are sent. Actually, on the whole, they are not usually sent that far because criminals are quite lazy about how far they'll go to take revenge. Eventually everybody went off to Australia *except* the crew. It was too expensive to send them, they just lost a job! Still, they went to Italy this year.'

So, having hit on an idea, what happens next?

'In the case of "Promised Land" they sent me out there for three weeks to do some research. I didn't want to set it in Sydney or Melbourne or any of the obvious places but to do a kind of western in fact. The idea was to take Morse away from his familiar territory, to see what happened when you took away his car, his beer, his music and in particular to see what happened to his relationship with Lewis because they really have to fall back on each other. I started with the fact that Lewis, of course, would absolutely love Australia and Morse would hate it. He is too old, he can't adjust, he's too cranky. He's not used to these people, they're very different. I knew that Morse would patronise them and practically get his nose punched for doing so, whereas Lewis would never have any of those snobbish attitudes. It was also a chance to give Lewis a degree of independence. I think the scene where he and the Australian policeman get drunk in the bar works like a dream. Usually Morse is in charge and Lewis, to some extent, has to hide how much he contributes. In this case he was going to be very much the man who knew how to make things work.

'I don't normally do story-lines. I discuss the ideas with the producer which leaves me with three or four pages of subject matter. I don't necessarily stick to them, they are just guidelines. Then I sit down and write the episode. "Masonic Mysteries" and "Promised Land" were quite fast. It all depends how much you have thought it out in advance. Even so there is never enough time. After you have submitted the script they come at you and tell you to rewrite it all. I don't usually get much beyond a third draft. The whole process takes between three and four months but you're doing other things in between.'

Mitchell started writing screenplays in the sixties. His first film was called *Arabesque* and, believe it or not, features an Oxford professor who becomes a target for assassination when he is asked by some oil-rich Arabs to decipher a hieroglyphic. It starred Sophia Loren and Gregory Peck. 'Twenty-four writers were working on it by the end,' recalls Mitchell, wryly. 'I learned then that if you write "medium-shot" the director will instantly shoot it in close-up or long-shot, that directors pay no attention to that kind of thing so you might as well forget it. In any case, most scenes are shot in all three then the editor, working closely with the director, will choose the shots and put them all together. It's completely useless saying what you want unless it's a crane or helicopter shot.

'At the start of "Masonic Mysteries" there's a wonderful crane shot but it wasn't my idea. When I was discussing the episode with Danny Boyle the director I could see he had a gleam in his eye so he obviously had it in mind all along. It's a terribly clever shot, very cinematic, very Hitchcockian. It looks like all one take but it is edited. Morse and his female passenger go past a street-lamp at one stage and come out the other side. There are various cheats but it is still very Hitchcockian. The director is very much the master of what you see on the screen but in English TV I'm always surprised how little they interfere with the script. In America they just change everything everyday so that it turns out completely different to what you intended.'

After writing fourteen hours of *Inspector Morse*, Mitchell feels that the detective is 'in my head now, it's a kind of kidnapping. Morse brings out my really gloomy side.' He laughs. 'I'm not really a gloomy person. To begin with I thought you had to be like the early cases, all death, death, death and excitement and puzzling and people sitting saying, "My God, yes, we should have thought of that." Actually you can be really slow in some ways. You can really talk about anything. You can do anything as long as you don't lose the story. I put in all sorts of things. With Morse and Lewis's relationship everything they say impinges on that

The writing process: how 'The Wolvercote Tongue' began. The first page of Colin Dexter's original storyline and (opposite) the corresponding page from Julian Mitchell's TV script.

① Double Alibi, by Colin Dexter

~~Theroute for Murder~~

~~Thirty~~

~~30.~~ American tourists, mostly from the ~~East~~ west coast (and predominantly Californians) — mostly, too, in the 60 – 75 age-bracket (a few younger ones, though) — are due in Oxford at 11 a.m. (see attached ~~Yellow Sheet~~).

We meet them as they drive in a luxury coach along the M 40. They are on a fortnight's holiday in ~~the~~ UK, for a Historic Cities of England Tour — on day ~~1~~ of this holiday, in fact. They have come from London where they spent two nights at the ~~Algonq~~ Waldorf Hotel (in the Aldwych). Twenty women; ten men; (& two or three husband-wife combinations). Most of the women are smoking, their richly-beringed and well manicured fingers favouring the inordinately long, king-sized Menthol cigarettes. These Women are pretty well educated (not at all the "where's the University?" type of ladies); and it becomes clear as we listen to their conversations that they have several most important things in common:

   — their husbands have retired (or have died)

   — They are rich

   — most are addicted to a daily diet of bridge — detective stories — tobacco —

   — They are all ~~xxxxxxxx~~ deeply & genuinely interested in the 'culture' of the Old World

Excalibur! Well, not exactly. It's the Wolvercote Tongue.

2

```
1.   EXT  OXFORD ST GILES/COACH/DAY                        1


It is nearly four o´clock on a fine summer afternoon.  Oxford
is looking splendid, and the trees are green in St Giles,
down which the usual traffic is pouring towards the Martyr´s
Memorial.  Among the cars and buses is a small luxury coach
with a travel company´s name on the outside.

2.   INT  COACH/ST GILES/DAY                              2

Inside the coach is a smallish group of American tourists,
mostly in their sixties and seventies.  Their guide is
sitting at the fron next to the DRIVER.  She is an attractive
Englishwoman in her mid-thirties, SHEILA WILLIAMS.  She has a
microphone.

                    SHEILA
          This street is called St Giles, and there´s
          been a Fair here every October since the Middle
          Ages.  The whole road´s blocked for days.

Among the TOURISTS we pick out HOWARD and SHIRLEY BROWN, a
cheerful couple in their sixties.

                    SHIRLEY
          How do people get around?

                    SHEILA
          They walk.

There is a general groan.

                    HOWARD
          Give us a break, Sheila!  My feet are
          killing me!

Opposite the BROWNS is JANET ROSCOE, a diminutive,
trouble-making, experienced traveller.  Next to her, and not
altogether sure he likes it, is PHIL ALDRICH, roughly the
same age---late sixties.  He has a very dry sense of humour.

                    JANET
          I should have liked longer at Waddeson
          myself.  Wouldn´t you, Phil?
```

relationship and develops it in one way or another. There is a lot of me in it yes, but I couldn't tell you how much. Morse is me and at the same time he isn't me. I have a lot of things in common with him. I suppose what I do is caricature parts of myself.'

When filming had been completed on 'The Wolvercote Tongue', which was first broadcast on Christmas Day 1987, Kenny McBain acknowledged the Dexter/Mitchell double act by giving each of them a piece of the beautiful Anglo-Saxon jewel. In reality the buckle and tongue were specially made for the film by Anthony Powell, the jeweller who designed Princess Diana's engagement ring. It cost £1200.

Dressed to kill? Morse at a dead end in 'The Dead of Jericho'.

ALMA CULLEN, whose legal drama series *Advocates* was screened on ITV last year, joined *Inspector Morse* for its third series and has contributed an episode a year ever since. Chris Burt, who had taken over from Kenny McBain, had produced Cullen's AIDS drama, *Intimate Contact*, and invited her to write 'The Secret of Bay 5B' from an outline by Colin Dexter. 'The Infernal Serpent' and 'Fat Chance' were based on her own ideas.

'Ideas are not a problem. You can pick up a newspaper every-day and see four incidents that could form the basis of an episode. It's welding those events into a story that is the difficult part. I don't mean to sound arrogant but I've a file of ideas. After a while you get a nose for them. The work comes in shaping those ideas within the format. To begin with it is not easy to fill a two-hour slot and to keep up the interest without going in for too much obfuscation and diverging from the main story. It's also extremely hard work providing dialogue for two such intelligent, gifted actors. Morse and Lewis have a special relationship, it's often witty. Keeping up the tone is hard.'

'The Infernal Serpent', which deals with the traumatic subject of child abuse, showed how well she had learned the ropes. Like Mitchell, Cullen works closely with the director. In this case it was John Madden. 'When he had read the script John told me he had a clear idea of what he wanted to do and it was perfect because he saw it the way I saw it. For instance, when the choir master decides to leave the country and writes a letter to Morse explaining his decision, we see him getting into a taxi outside the college while a voice-over reads out the letter. John went to great lengths to get an overhead shot in this scene so that, as the cab pulls away, we see a KEEP CLEAR sign on the road. Perhaps some of the viewers did not notice this, perhaps it only registered subliminally, but the sign is a motif of the character as a whole. These little things do count.'

If further proof were necessary that such details are not acci-dental, we need look no further than the very first minute of the very first episode of *Inspector Morse*. As Morse pulls up in front of the garage a large sign fills the centre of the screen. Red letters on a white background spell out NO EXIT. Morse's car is about to get smashed and will be going nowhere. The episode, 'The Dead of Jericho', takes place for the most part in Canal Reach, the cul-de-sac where Anne Stavely lives and dies. In more ways than one it is a dead end.

'The Dead of Jericho' also features a swimming pool. When Mrs Richards gets up in the night to replace the umbrella in the back of the car, she scuttles along the side of an empty pool. Although each episode is a film in its own right, this sign of wealth and leisure for some reason crops up again and again in *Inspector*

Pooling of resources: Morse and Lewis contemplate the solution to the mystery of 'The Sins of the Fathers'.

Morse. 'The Sins of the Fathers' and 'Fat Chance' feature full ones, the latter with the dubious added attraction of synchronised swimming; 'Greeks Bearing Gifts' features an almost empty one; 'Last Seen Wearing' shows one on video and 'Promised Land', an episode in which everything is on a much greater scale, has an Olympic-sized one with only a young girl in it. Perhaps it's because the characters are nearly always out of their depth. Whatever the reason, the viewer has no difficulty immersing him or herself in the film.

Sometimes, though, luck does play a part. 'When John took me to the college chapel that they had found for the climax of "The Infernal Serpent",' says Cullen, 'I liked it immediately and said, "Yes, this is it." "Look at the windows," said John. I did and

saw that the stained-glass in one window depicted a serpent in the garden of Eden and, in another, there was actually an animal's skull similar to the sheep's head that appears in the photograph that contains the answer to the mystery.' That's what you call a godsend.

After the episode had been transmitted Cullen received a letter from a woman who had been abused as a child in similar circumstances. 'It was very poignant. She told me how, just like the Cheryl Campbell character, she had wanted to confront the man who was still widely respected and say, "You did this to me, you took a part of my childhood away," but found it impossible. As the plot unfolded she knew from her own experiences what the ending would be.'

Dear departed: the funeral of Dr Dear in 'The Infernal Serpent'. It was shot in the chapel of University College, where director John Madden had found the perfect temptation scene in one of the stained-glass windows.

'T HE idea for "Driven to Distraction" dropped through my letter-box,' says Anthony Minghella who, in addition to three episodes of *Inspector Morse*, has written widely for stage and screen. His works include *Whale Music*, *What If It's Raining?* and *Madly, Truly, Deeply*. 'I live in the London borough of Islington and I received a brochure on crime prevention. I read it and came across this paragraph which said, "If you are a woman driving home alone and you feel that you are being followed, stick to main roads." I thought, how preposterous! What happens if you don't live on a main road? Then I thought, my God, something like this must only be included because women are being followed home. I saw how easy it would be to sit in a car, see a woman driving, and follow her.

'When writing for *Morse* you can't allow yourself to think that anybody else is ever going to write for the characters again. A certain amount of appropriation goes on. You have to believe that Morse and Lewis can articulate your own concerns, that you inhabit them and don't have to make any adjustment to your taste. It's no good saying, I don't like Wagner but we better have it because Morse does. There's nothing in it about genre to me. It's a question of writing the best thing you can write at the time.

'I carry a very pathetic world view. Murder is so inhumane that I find it almost impossible to accept that a crime outside of a crime of passion is possible by somebody who is in full control of their faculties.'

In 'Deceived by Flight' Sharon Maughan plays Kate Donn who kills her husband. 'The day after it was shown,' says Minghella, 'she and Kevin Whately appeared on a phone-in programme. A woman rang Sharon to say, "You were so nice, my husband and I really liked you and we were so disappointed that you'd done it." Sharon then said, "I don't think I did do it." Kevin gave her this look and she continued, "With all due respect to Anthony Minghella, I don't think that I could have done it." Amazing.'

Opposite *Sitting on a fortune: Morse arrests Barker in 'Deceived by Flight'. A consignment of drugs is hidden in the wheelchair.*

CHAPTER SEVEN

THE SHOOT

First impressions are often misleading
'LAST BUS TO WOODSTOCK'

I T takes a vast amount of organisation and sheer hard work to make a series of *Inspector Morse*. If everybody involved were to be mentioned during the closing credits – at least one hundred – the programme would never end.

Every episode goes through three main phases. Television folk refer to these as pre-production, production and post-production. To the rest of us this translates as planning, shooting and completing.

Once it is decided that another series is to be made – in an ideal world this would be six months before filming were due to begin – the executive producer, the producer and the head of the script department meet to commission the story-lines. If the series is to consist of five episodes, six of these detailed outlines are commissioned so that there is a margin for error.

'In film-making terms, the executive producer is usually the person who comes up with the money or the person representing the people who came up with the money,' says Ted Childs. 'In television they are often the head of the department which originated the series. I am the person with editorial and managerial responsibility. In other words if *Inspector Morse* were a newspaper I would be its editor. I'm the one who gets fired if it goes radically wrong and, in my turn, I can fire all the people who work on it below me.' He laughs. 'The buck stops here.

'I play a big part in the scripts because I enjoy doing that. Our script man Tim Whitby – who took over from Patrick Harbinson – the producer, Zenith and myself decide what we do and do not like about them and give the go-ahead to the best five. We're in the happy position now of people coming forward and offering to write for *Morse*. It's a very difficult genre to write in. There have been a number of very good dramatists – who shall remain nameless – who found difficulty with crime fiction drama. They could either plot very well but their characters were cardboard or equally they came up with wonderful characters but the plot didn't hold up. It's not simply a question of talent.'

When the writers have been decided upon, the producer assumes control of the day-to-day running of the production. For the fourth and fifth series this was David Lascelles, the longest-serving producer of the series to date, who is also a viscount and in line to the British throne.

Opposite In the driving seat: Michael Davis (front centre), director of photography, at work on 'The Last Enemy'.

'A producer doesn't do anything on his own but he does a bit of everybody else's job,' says Lascelles. 'The next stage, as far as I was concerned, was to find directors who could put their own stamp on the series. I set out to emphasise that each *Morse* is a feature film. Television directors are too often servants of the text. I tried to make interesting marriages between writers and directors, to create combinations that you normally wouldn't think of. The most successful I achieved in the fourth series was that between Julian Mitchell and Danny Boyle on "Masonic Mysteries". Although they both have theatrical backgrounds, Danny has an iconoclastic side to him. His toughness with the material compensates for Julian's tendency to be over-jokey at times. They got on like a house on fire.' Indeed, they burned out Morse's flat.

Just as Childs believes that 'you've got to give people the scope to get on with things', Lascelles did not personally choose every single person who worked on the series. 'Each producer appoints his own production team – i.e. the film editor, the costume designer, the production designer, the lighting cameraman and the sound man – but they, in turn, as heads of their departments, recruit their own colleagues. It's important that they should work with people whom they know and trust and want around them.'

Casting sessions usually take place in the presence of the producer, the director and, if possible, the writer. Everyone entertains certain ideas about how each character should be but a compromise is generally reached. An actor's appearance, ability and reputation all play a part. Mistakes are seldom made. For instance, it's hard not to see mischief in 'Deceived by Flight', when Kate Donn, played by Sharon Maughan, star of the Gold Blend commercials, says at one point, 'It's coffee, I hate coffee.' It says much for the quality of the series – and the scripts – that it attracts brilliant performances from the likes of James Grout, Sir Michael Hordern, Patricia Hodge, Barry Foster, Lionel Jeffries, Zoë Wanamaker and Maurice Denham.

Where they are going to do it matters just as much as who is going to do it. This is the responsibility of the producer and the location manager. In considering any site, the aesthetics have to be balanced with the logistics. Because each episode is filmed in five weeks – that's only twenty-five working days – and nearly all of it is shot on location, this calls for detailed forward-planning. The scenes of any script are not shot in chronological order because this would waste a great deal of time and money. All the scenes in one location are filmed before the crew move on to another.

Many episodes require at least a couple of scenes in an Oxford college. Even though every effort is made to minimise the effects of shooting, a film crew causes disruption. The fewer people there are on a set the better. Consequently filming is restricted towards

the end of the long summer vacation because many colleges hold summer schools as soon as the students have returned home. Generally speaking, only one of the five weeks is spent in Oxford but there are exceptions. In 'The Infernal Serpent' most of the action takes place within a single college – its quads and chapel, the Master's lodge – and so three weeks were required. However – and you should never take anything at face value in *Morse* – because of the very precise nature of the setting, for example, a study overlooking the garden, the features of *two* colleges, University College and Merton, had to be stitched together to make one. For the following episode, 'The Sins of the Fathers', all that was needed were 'second unit drive-bys'. In other words, a second film crew shot the footage (Oxford exteriors, landmarks and skylines) which was needed to establish where Morse was supposed to be and to provide links in the narrative. The 'real' filming was going on elsewhere.

Not a single frame of 'Masonic Mysteries' was shot in Oxford. St Albans, not for the first time, served as a picturesque stand-in. In the fifth series the police station was in Harrow. For the first four series it was a converted Territorial Army hall in Southall which has since been demolished. Morse's flat is actually in north London. 'Ealing [in west London] looks like a lot of suburban Oxford,' says Lascelles. 'It was practically built at the same time. Those big redbrick houses set back from the road are very

Photo finish: Maurice Denham as Mandeville in the lair of the lunatic Reverend Geoffrey Boyd.

Crew cut: the men behind the camera on 'The Last Enemy'.

characteristic of the streets off Woodstock Road. This is very useful if you have lots of ex-BBC crew members because many of them live there. They can go home for breakfast.'

Occasionally, though, a studio is necessary: you can't burn down people's houses. 'It was not possible to do the fire in Morse's flat in ''Masonic Mysteries'' as strongly as we wanted so we had to build a double of the living room in a studio. It wasn't worth shooting a single scene inside so we organised a week's shooting around it. There is no upstairs in the real flat so we had to construct one. This enabled us to film from above when Lewis climbs the stairs to the bathroom.'

After a day's shooting the film is sent to be developed and by mid-morning the next day the director and the producer are able to look at the 'rushes' and to check that the footage is up to scratch. 'Once they're shooting, the crew should be allowed to get on with it,' says Lascelles. 'They know what is expected of them so I only visit the set if I think it is going to be a difficult day, i.e. if there is to be a night shoot, a crowd scene or a dangerous stunt.'

As filming continues the editor is already at work assembling the rushes into the correct time sequence. When the shoot is over and all the pieces have been put together the result is known as a 'rough assembly'. The director and the editor, with the advice of the producer, then have two weeks to choose the shots they want for each scene and to create a film that is more or less the correct length. This is known as 'the director's cut'. The film is then shown to the executive producer, Ted Childs, and other executives. If any changes are agreed they are carried out and the picture 'locked off' – that is, no further changes can be made – and it is then known as 'the final cut'. But there still remains a lot of work to be done.

The sound engineers have three weeks to do what is known as the track-laying. This involves breaking down the sound into its basic ingredients: footsteps, birdsong, dialogue, etc. If the words are still not distinct enough after they have been cleaned up it is possible for the actors to re-record the lines in question. It is at this stage that the extra sound is added: background voices, telephones, sirens, the crackle of walkie-talkies. 'It is a very fiddly business,' says Lascelles. 'For the fifth series we used a digital system for the first time and it made a considerable difference. For instance, with ''Promised Land'', we could broadcast in stereo, something that we had never done before.' Meanwhile, Barrington Pheloung, working from the final cut, composes the music. It is recorded in one day and mixed on the next. Then, in a dubbing session which lasts about a week and a half, all the sound is mixed together. The very last stage is when the film is transferred on to videotape.

One of the main reasons why *Inspector Morse* looks so good is because it has been filmed on 16 mm film rather than on videotape. This increases the cost of shooting an episode by 15 per cent. In addition, because technology is improving all the time, this has meant that each series has looked better than the one before. This may seem difficult to understand but it is not. David Lascelles explains.

'*Inspector Morse* is shot on negative. Usually a print is made and that's what you work with, cutting it up, putting marks on it, sellotaping it back together. The negative is not touched. When the picture is finished, locked off, you go back to the negative and, using the number on each frame, match it to the final cut. This is done by hand by a man wearing white gloves in an hermetically sealed room. The negative is cut into two rolls, an A roll and a B roll, so that shots one, three, five, seven, etc, are on roll A and shots two, four, six, eight, etc, are on roll B with black spaces in the gaps. This enables you to dissolve between shots. If you literally just joined all the shots together on one roll you would have little bumps and white flashes every time it cut. You can see this in old programmes such as *Monty Python's Flying Circus*. For example the filmed inserts of Cleese and company running through the woods, sheep exploding all about them, are very jerky.'

Once the two rolls have been completed the colour-grading

has to be done. This process enables the colour of every single shot to be adjusted by hand. It takes the technician, and the producer and director, two days to do a single episode. It is an important stage, and one where creative decisions are made. For instance, two characters in the same scene may have been lit differently. The director might want a scene to be slightly darker or lighter than it appears, or to increase the contrast within it. Ideally the lighting cameraman should also be present but, more often than not, he is already shooting the next episode. As they are made, all these instructions are fed into a computer shot by shot by shot. Then the two rolls of film are transferred on to the videotape with their alterations and the titles added electronically. Originally the titles were filmed separately and spliced into the tape.

So what are the benefits of all this painstaking work? For a start it is the use of 16 mm film that creates the soft, grainy blue light that is one of the hallmarks of the series: headlights glowing gold in the dusk, the yellow stone of a college shining against the blue sky, rain glistening at night. It adds gloss, polish, sheen. As Sylvie says in 'The Infernal Serpent', 'the visuals seem almost too good to miss'.

'With this way,' insists Lascelles, 'you're getting the best of both worlds. Video tends to want to make things look like video. It flattens things out. You lose the contrast, depth and mystery of film. It sounds pretentious but film has a mystery to it. It's certainly there. Even the untutored, untechnical eye can tell the difference.'

One down, four episodes to go – except that the schedule just described is not followed consecutively but concurrently. 'By the middle of the production year you'll have reached a point where film three will be actually being shot, film one will be in the very last stages of colour-grading, film two will be in the editing suite, film four will be in preparation and film five will probably still be in the process of being written. Some days I'd be almost speechless by the evening. It is mind-boggling.' The sixth series, for instance, was shot between mid-May and the end of November 1991.

The order of shooting is not necessarily the order of transmission. 'The former is a juggling act, really, that depends on a number of things,' Lascelles explains. 'The availability of writers and directors, access to locations and the requirements of the script. For instance, because a lot of "Masonic Mysteries" happens at night, it made sense to shoot it last, during the autumn, when there was less daylight. As for the order of screening that's up to you. Although the episodes are not conceived as sequential, I thought it important to create the illusion of progression, that the characters have gone through some sort of change. It's always good to leave Morse in a darker and lonelier place than he has ever been before.'

THERE comes a point when the script has to be turned into reality, when the theory has to be put into practice. What follows is a privileged peep behind the scenes of two productions of *Inspector Morse*.

Two director's chairs sit on the lawn of a quad in Magdalen College, Oxford. The closely cropped grass is as green and smooth as the baize on a brand-new snooker table. Above looms the tower of the college chapel, described by the art historian Sir Nikolaus Pevsner as the most beautifully proportioned in all England.

It is 1990. September is giving way to October. Michaelmas term has yet to begin, the students have yet to arrive. Only a few tourists wander about the quiet precincts. From an open window on the first floor drifts a single word: 'Cut!'

Conversation breaks out. A couple of moments later someone slowly descends the stone staircase and emerges into the sun-filled court. It is John Thaw. He strolls over to one of the chairs and lights a cigarette.

Upstairs in the ancient library another scene of 'Greeks Bearing Gifts' is being set up. A miniature railway runs over the gleaming

One for the road: setting up a driving shot during the making of 'Ghost in the Machine'.

Make-up man: Robin Grantham, John Thaw and Kevin Whately on an Italian job.

floorboards and down the central aisle. The vaulted ceiling is lit to emphasise its fine plasterwork. Cables snake all over the place. A host of men and women, most of them in T-shirts and jeans, attend to various pieces of equipment. Walkie-talkies spit static at each other. Although the windows are open it is hot in the chamber. A portly college porter, there to see that no damage is done, sits on a wooden stool and mops his brow. Snow-topped Richard Pearson, who plays Jerome Hogg, is having his make-up re-touched. He returns to his position behind a large desk that is situated in a bay at the far end of the library. Down below, the college gardens look magnificent.

John Thaw returns to the fray. Inspector Morse is here to find out what Hogg knows about the members of a symposium on Greek maritime history that met last year in Piraeus. Did everybody behave themselves?

'Hanky-panky? Hello sailor? There's a lot less of that than in the good old days. I suppose I'm lucky, sowed my oats before the scourge came. Now I'm an old man the hunger's abated somewhat.' As Pearson delivers these lines he gets up and begins to walk down the aisle. The camera dollies back on its tracks. The rest of the crew shrink back into the book-lined alcoves. On the screen it appears that Morse and Hogg are quite alone.

The next task is to film Morse asking his questions from the front. Although Thaw simply has to sit down and place a cup of coffee on the desk it is a complex shot. It is rehearsed; Adrian Shergold, the director, advises the actors, then they go for a take. They shoot it again and again and again. Each time the cup is emptied out then re-filled with fresh coffee from a Thermos so that the swirling steam will be visible on the film. The stylist adjusts Thaw's hair. Make-up, costume and continuity people hover. The sound and lighting men wait.

It becomes clear that the star of the series is becoming irritated. During the next take he lets it show. A hint of steel slides into his voice. 'Perfect,' says Shergold and he's right. After all Morse *is* annoyed that Hogg is deliberately not giving anything away. Somewhere, as if on cue, a piano practice begins.

It has taken the best part of an afternoon to shoot a scene that will last about a minute on television. The crew pack their gear away. The library is returned to its former glory. The minder looks relieved. Outside the director's chairs are folded up and carried off.

Because the next scene has to be shot at night the team can take time out. The caterers have discreetly parked down a back street, away from prying eyes. The crew eat their food next door in a coach. Thaw and his director have returned to the Randolph Hotel.

Shergold, whose other work includes *Close Relations*, *Goodbye Cruel World* and Dennis Potter's *Christabel*, also directed 'Second Time Around' in the fifth series.

'I used to be an actor before I became a director and had appeared in *The Sweeney* with John. I didn't expect him to remember me but he did. He reminds me of a kindly uncle. He has an extraordinary screen presence. I've seen actors quiver when they meet him. He has an enormous knowledge of the film industry and creates an atmosphere on the set. When you're rehearsing a scene with him he'll know where to stand in a room out of sheer instinct. He knows everybody's job. He knows if the grip (the man who pushes the camera) is hitting his marks, he knows if the focus-puller is doing it right, he knows if the camera operator is operating properly and he knows if the director has done his homework. This encourages everyone to come up to scratch.'

With such a tight schedule it's not easy waiting for it to get dark. Shergold doffs his red LA baseball cap and puts it back on again. 'It takes ages to light for night.'

LATE July 1991. The penultimate day of shooting on 'The Death of the Self', the second film in the production schedule for series six. Harefield, Hertfordshire, is standing in for Verona, Italy. That's why an Italian policeman is strolling in the English sun.

It wasn't meant to be this way. The past month has been spent on location in Italy but foreign filming creates all sorts of problems. For instance, the humid temperatures were too much for some of the cast, who fainted. Because of custom controls and the distances involved, rushes took two days to be developed instead of one. It was only after the crew had left Verona that they discovered that one of the lenses had been faulty with the result that a crucial shot was 'soft' (out of focus). Consequently a prefabricated garage in the grounds of the deserted Ministry of Defence laboratory being used as this year's police station has been transformed into a fifteenth-century courtyard in Verona with the aid of two plastic ionic columns.

The director, designer and lighting cameraman consult each other on the best way to trick the eye. Barry, John Thaw's stocky body-double, steps forwards and backwards as instructed so that the correct position for Morse to stand in can be worked out. The spot is then marked with strips of tape.

Sound-mixer Tony Dawe, seated on a white wooden folding chair and cushion, stops the tape and prepares for the next take. He worked with Thaw on *Redcap* and on every episode of *The Sweeney*. He turned down the chance to work on Ridley Scott's new film *Christopher Columbus* starring Gerard Depardieu, to do another series of *Inspector Morse*. 'I'm in charge of recording all the dialogue and background sound effects for each episode. I make sure everybody can hear what the actors are saying. With *Morse* you know that you're going to have a good time and produce a good product. This is what it's all about. I know that virtually all my work will end up on the screen – with a feature film only ten to fifteen per cent survives.'

Dawe received Oscar nominations for his work on *Return of the Jedi, Empire of the Sun, Who Framed Roger Rabbit?* and *Indiana Jones and the Last Crusade*. Compared with Oxford, Italy proved to be 'incredibly noisy'. 'The Italians live on the street. It's impossible to beat the noise, you have to go with it and produce a film full of colour and the flavour of the place. Even when we got to what we thought was a quiet courtyard there would be televisions blaring out, snatches of music, doors banging and people chattering away in Italian. And then there were the German tourists.'

The change in scenery prompts Morse to change his clothes, too. While in Italy he buys himself a linen suit. It was wardrobe master Tony Allen who came up with the idea.

'I'm responsible for all the costumes that the actors wear. The

costume designer and myself decide on what they are going to wear in each scene and I go out and buy them and make sure they fit,' says Allen, who trained as a tailor. He entered the film industry as a driver and a stunt-man and worked with Thaw on *The Sweeney*. 'It sounds easy but it isn't. We have to make out a dress chart for each character because, as we don't shoot in sequence, you have to know what each actor is wearing on each day. It's a question of continuity. You have to remember how the knot of a tie looked three weeks ago, whether or not the top button of the shirt was undone and so on. If you don't know your script you can make terrible mistakes. For instance, it's my job to know if four identical outfits will be needed for a particular stunt. After that it's the washing, ironing and general tidying up.'

All these chores take place in the back of a specially converted coach. The seating area has been replaced with hanging space for the clothes required by every character in the film, plus drawers and cupboards for shoes. One carrier bag contains a selection of policemen's helmets. The rear of the vehicle has been turned into a kitchen complete with fitted washing machine and drier. These were forced into overtime in Verona where the temperature was over 120 degrees Fahrenheit. Even so, in between takes, the cast had to place wads of tissue under their arms to stop the sweat staining their clothes.

The wardrobe wagon is just one of a large number of cars, caravans and lorries that are parked on the far side of the derelict mansion in whose grounds the MOD built their ugly base. The branches of a massive ancient yew tree droop right down on to the overgrown lawn. When the crew break for lunch it is as if the circus has come to town. A queue forms by the catering truck. The menu today is liver and onions, turkey curry or omelette. John Thaw retires to his trailer. Kevin Whately goes to the salad bar instead and, sitting on the top floor of the double-decker dining room, talks about his part in 'The Death of the Self'.

'This time round Lewis actually goes out and has a good time with an American lady. At first he doesn't want to get involved and resists her – he doesn't like Italy, it's much more foreign to him than Australia, he wants to be at home – but then he sees there's no reason why he shouldn't have some fun.'

Tummy full, Whately goes to change into his pyjamas. The next scene to be shot in the garage is set in the hotel in Italy. In reality it is two pieces of plasterboard, one of which has a built-in door. Fresh flowers in a vase on a table by Lewis's room add to the illusion.

'You don't go all the way to Italy to shoot interiors,' says Peter Greenhalgh, director of photography, whose previous commission was *Soldier, Soldier*. 'With an ordinary episode of *Morse* set in England about sixty per cent of it would be shot inside. Most of the Italian one, like the Australian one, is shot outside. As director of photography you're responsible for the whole look of the film from start to finish. I'm not a lighting technician but I decide on which lights are needed to produce the right effect. You have to be faithful to the look of the series – with five different directors it is important to provide some consistency. The public would be mighty surprised if one film looked like a comic strip and the other four did

not – but each director wants to emphasise a certain aspect of it and the DOP discusses this with them. I've tried to make *Morse* look slightly more contrasty, slightly more gritty, to give it a slightly more real edge. You have to be inventive visually because there are few stunts. If the camera didn't keep moving you'd be left with a lot of static shots of people talking to each other. The DOP works closely with the director but, in technical terms, he has the final say in how something will look on the screen.'

As well as 'The Death of the Self' Colin Gregg also directed 'Who Killed Harry Field?' which contains one of the best shots in the whole canon of *Inspector Morse*. The fact that Lewis is hoping for promotion, that their working relationship could soon be at an end, depresses Morse. Called to a country pub where Harry's motorbike has been found, he wanders across the road into an open cornfield that stretches as far as the eye can see. The flatness is only broken by a distant oak tree silhouetted against the grey sky. Thunder rumbles. Morse, a man alone, stands, hands in pockets, with his back to the camera. It is a wonderful moment. Lewis joins him. 'Something happened here,' says Morse. The viewer agrees.

Does anything similar happen in 'The Death of the Self'?

'I think so,' says Gregg with a quick grin. 'In the opera house the set for *Turandot* contains these green-painted clouds. We did

Arena of conflict: director Colin Gregg and John Thaw on the shoot of 'The Death of the Self'.

this lovely tracking shot past them to Frances Barber and John Thaw. It was perfect for her character because she exists in a world of unreality, everything about her – where she lives, her life-style, the kind of person that she is – are all one step removed from reality. The set symbolised that and buried in it was Morse. Outside forces had come in and put their own design on the film. Suddenly the image said more than the words. I try to make this happen as much as possible.'

Writer Alma Cullen describes the episode as 'a cappuccino, frothy on top but dark underneath'. What follows evidently belongs to the dark bit. Morse has been bashed on the head, and, thanks to the make-up man, his scalp is sticky with blood. All that needs to be shot is for Morse to reach Lewis's room, knock on the door and be taken in. A few moments before Gregg says 'action', Thaw stands by one of the lights with his eyes closed. The camera begins to roll. He staggers to the door, raps his knuckles on it then leans back against the door jamb. Lewis opens the door. 'Bloody hell!' He brings Morse inside and closes the door. 'Cut.' They don't need to do it again.

As the crew move to another part of the complex to set up a crown-shaped cauldron, the flames of which will open the film, Thaw sits on his own director's chair and describes what he was doing in the previous scene.

'This sounds awfully pretentious but it isn't. I was imagining what it would be like to be hit on the back of the head, being semi-conscious for a while, getting into the car and driving back to the hotel from the countryside.'

Was his head hurting? He laughs. 'Well, in a way it was. You feel as if it is. Logic comes into it too. The guy would move slowly, he would be stunned. His balance would be shaky, he would have a terrible headache. His head would be throbbing but I couldn't put my hand to my head and groan like a bad actor. You have to do it all inside somehow.'

Thaw has finished for the day. His driver is waiting to take him home. There are lines to be learned before going to bed. And tomorrow, just like any other day, the car will be back to collect him at 6.30 a.m.

Opposite Opera lover: Frances Barber and Co. on the set of 'Turandot', complete with green clouds.

CHAPTER EIGHT

THREE OF
THE BEST

You were being quite intelligent then, go on
'SERVICE OF ALL THE DEAD'

'SERVICE OF ALL THE DEAD', the third and final episode of the first series, was originally broadcast on 20 January 1987. Written by Julian Mitchell from Colin Dexter's book, and directed by Peter Hammond, it is in many ways the most complex film in the entire canon of *Inspector Morse*. It is also one of the best.

The episode begins with a distant, hazy view of Oxford's dreaming spires. Bells are ringing. They might be calling the faithful to prayer but they are also calling us to a murder. By means of a series of overlapping shots, the camera sweeps across the city's skyline and comes to rest on the tower of St Oswald's. We drop to ground level. In the graveyard an arm falls out from behind a tombstone. Organ music draws us inside the church where all the main characters are. By the time the opening titles are finished someone has been killed in the vestry. Any dreams have turned to nightmares. The bells are in fact a death knell.

Although the plot is an ingenious one – it turns out that Harry Josephs, the person assumed to have been the first victim, is in fact the killer – it is only part of the reason why the film is so enjoyable. The escalating body-count is certainly satisfying, and given Morse's passion for crosswords, 'Six Down' would have been an equally apt title. But the real pleasure of 'Service of all the Dead' is the way in which the style and the script complicate and complement each other.

'Always best to throw light on the scene if you can,' says Morse as he enters the murk of the church. Sunshine streams through the stained-glass windows. The interior is a kaleidoscope of reds, greens, purples and yellows, but the prettiness soon degenerates into luridness. It is odd that *stained* glass should be an integral part of a church, a place of sanctity and purity. St Oswald's, though, has been defiled. Blood is staining the vestry. The Communion wine, the blood of Christ, contains 'enough morphine to kill an elephant'. As Morse points out, the drug must have been administered in a poisoned chalice.

'I don't like this kind of church,' comments Morse. The gruesome representation of Christ's suffering – his crown of thorns, the nails driven through his hands and feet – and that of St Sebastian,

Opposite Heaven's above: a brother of Christ contemplates fratricide.

Mass murder: the vicar of St Oswald's prays for success.

pierced by arrows, is enough to make anyone squeamish. But 'Service of all the Dead' is about agony and the lengths to which people will go to escape it. The vicar is being blackmailed, Josephs' wife is an adulteress, Ruth Rawlinson is in thrall to her invalid mother who, forced to enter a nursing home at the close, is told by a brusque nurse, 'We all have our crosses to bear.'

The whole episode centres on the single word 'cross'. The two main themes are religion and crosswords. Churches are laid out in the shape of a cross. The first victim is stabbed with a Cross-of-Christ letter opener. It is when Morse sees a crossword on the seat of his superior's car that he realises that S. O. Pawlen, the vicar, is an anagram of Swanpole, the tramp, who is his brother. The word for the answer entered into a crossword grid is 'light'. In other words, he sees the light. He has been at cross purposes. The floor of the church is paved with old gravestones. A close-up of one of them reveals that it is decorated with a skull and crossbones. The film is full of such details.

When Morse answers the telephone in Part Three, the hall is filled with the reflection of stained-glass. When Ruth is in bed with Harry in Part Four, reflections from stained-glass play on the white sheets. In Part Two the path lab glows with a green light. When

Morse and Lewis dash to St Oswald's for the final showdown the screen is suddenly filled with the startling close-up of a red traffic light. Danger lies ahead.

In *Inspector Morse* there is no such thing as coincidence. When the first victim is found, one of the corpse's arms is flung out in a similar manner to the one that emerged from behind the headstone in the graveyard. The vicar, having thrown himself from the top of the tower, lands on a bicycle in a position – arms akimbo, knees bent – that deliberately mirrors the crucifixion. When Mrs Josephs is found dead in the rowing boat her right arm lies in the now familiar pose. When Morse is attacked on the roof of the tower he also falls in the same way.

Peter Hammond's direction makes full use of reflections, sometimes to a dizzying degree (but then he does conclude with a tribute to Hitchcock's *Vertigo*). A car bonnet, a bookie's window, a motor-cycle wing-mirror, a car's rear-view mirror and a handbag mirror are just some of the surfaces used to reflect the action. Even the vicar's glasses are exploited. This isn't just a question of being tricksy. Time and time again we are shown that appearances are deceptive, that things are not what they seem. In a symmetrical crossword grid one half is the same as the other half except that it

Signal failure: Victor Preece, the murderous mummy's boy in 'Sins of the Fathers'. Director Peter Hammond shoots the moment when Morse nails Preece through the coloured glass of the signal as it changes from green to red. A similar shot occurs in his 'Service of all the Dead' when we see an extreme close-up of a set of traffic lights. Red means danger.

'I don't like this kind of church': Morse at cross purposes in 'Service of all the Dead'.

is *the other way round*. Morse learns that the tramp was not the killer but the killed.

Symmetry is used in other ways too. The taking of Communion is cross-cut with winos getting drunk outside. The discovery of Peter Morris's corpse in the crypt (a cryptic clue if ever there was one) is cross-cut with the finding of Josephs' dead wife. The boy's golden hair, which we saw the vicar ruffling fondly earlier, peeps out from the black coke. The woman's hair flows over the side of the boat. It is the same colour as the boy's.

If this all seems like critical over-kill perhaps it should be emphasised that 'Service of all the Dead' is both amusing and exciting. The episode is awash with booze. The Communion wine is lethal, Swanpole is an alcoholic, Ruth's mother is a sherry addict, Lewis is able to get confidential information from a bank because the manager drinks in Morse's pub and the two policemen only think of looking for Peter beneath St Oswald's when the barman says that he'll have to fetch a new cask from the cellar. When the

Opposite *Watch out, it's raining vicars: Morse saves Ruth from an unholy death.*

Cycle of destruction:
Pawlen has fallen. Note
the way his position
resembles a crucifixion.

case is finally solved, and Morse has almost been strangled, he glumly tells Lewis, 'I'm off the beer.' The unholy goings-on in the House of God that initially filled the viewer with such glee end up leaving a bad taste in the mouth.

For the climax of the episode we return to the top of the tower which we first saw at the start of the programme. John Thaw magnificently portrays the swooning nausea of someone who suffers from vertigo. Nevertheless, Morse, no doubt regretting his earlier joke about 'high mass murder', pursues Josephs on to the roof. It was the end of the series – at the time the audience didn't know whether there would be a second one. Would Morse die? Of course not. As always, Sergeant Lewis, brandishing a candlestick – a typical *Cluedo* weapon – saves his colleague, and Josephs plummets from the tower.

However the episode closes half underground. Morse – 'Chastity and continence, when did I ever have anything else?' – falls for Ruth and is even economical with the truth to mitigate the case against her. When she has been sentenced he visits her in her cell. The sun streams through the high window which is criss-crossed with bars. They embrace standing in the middle of the empty room. It is a moving scene and one of desolation. Still, it ends with a kiss. And what symbol signifies a kiss? X.

Where the hell are we?
'PROMISED LAND'

'PROMISED LAND', the fifth and final episode of the fifth series, was originally broadcast on 20 March 1991. Much of the power of *Inspector Morse* comes from the way it exploits Oxford's claustrophobic atmosphere of worlds within worlds, of enclosed, secretive, communities. However, this film, written by Julian Mitchell and directed by John Madden, takes Morse, Lewis and the series itself into new territory.

Following the AIDS-related death of Peter Matthews in prison, an inquiry is launched into the case of the Abingdon Gang. Morse, who was in charge of the investigation, has to travel to Hereford to interview Mike Harding, the supergrass whose evidence put the men away. That's Hereford, New South Wales. Morse, of course, wants Lewis to accompany him: 'I can't carry my own bags, can I?' Lewis is not too disappointed because, inevitably, he has cousins in NSW.

The whole episode plays on the conflict between the old and the new. Australians call England the 'Old Country'. When the policemen fly out it is raining. Down Under the sun never stops shining. Morse cannot cope with the new environment. Sweating profusely in his suit and tie, pestered by flies, he is even unable to use the air-conditioning unit in the motel. Lewis, suitably dressed in shorts and short-sleeved shirt, has to work it for him. Morse doesn't like barbecues – he can't cook and is not allowed to eat steak – but Lewis loves them. As Mitchell cruelly robs Morse of all his props – he forgets his music, he has to leave his car behind and is forced to drink orange juice ('They don't spell Australian beer with four Xs out of ignorance'), he has to rely on Lewis more and more. This dependence is at its heaviest just before the climax of the film when, for the first time in twenty episodes, Morse calls Lewis by his first name. 'How old are you?' asks Lewis. Morse sighs. 'I forget, Robbie.' In 'Promised Land' John Thaw gives his best performance (so far).

Both Morse and Anne Harding (Rhondda Findleton), wife of the supergrass, find that it is impossible to escape from the past. Mike and his family came halfway round the world to start a new life but, as Anne tells Morse, 'You saved him from one sort of prison but you condemned us both to another. Sentence for life. A real old-fashioned marriage.' Morse is married to his job. In 'Masonic Mysteries' he insists, 'I never put anyone away who wasn't guilty, never.' But in this episode he discovers that Matthews was innocent and that Harding had lied to protect himself. Morse crumbles: 'Oh my God.' You'll never see a better acted scene on TV.

The past catches up with the Hardings when the brother of the dead man (Con O'Neill) tracks them down. The avenger provides much of the dramatic tension. He is outside the nursing home when Morse and Lewis turn up to find that Anne's mother has been attacked. Lewis, who wishes to examine the brown camper-van driven by Matthews, is about to approach it – and Matthews is reaching for a gun – when Morse stops him, thus unwittingly saving his life. It is usually Lewis who gets Morse out of trouble.

The camper-van is visible in the background on at least a couple of occasions but the characters remain oblivious to it until Lewis recognises its driver on a videotape of the funeral with which the episode begins. Mitchell is fond of technological betrayal. In 'Ghost in the Machine' John McKendrick is found out when Lewis retrieves from the word-processor in Lord Hanbury's study the suicide note that the gardener had concocted. Computers and cameras play a vital part in 'Masonic Mysteries' too. In 'The Promised Land' John Madden's direction, as well as the physical action, builds up the sense of approaching nemesis.

'This isn't an Oxford college,' says Lewis as Morse flounders. A member of the Thames Valley force has no jurisdiction in Australia. 'It's so empty,' says Morse of Oz. The sense of space is unnerving. Madden emphasises this with a succession of wide, horizontal images. A tiny plane landing on a strip in the Outback . . . A deserted swimming pool which, in its bright composition of aquamarine water, green grass, palm trees and azure sky, resembles a David Hockney . . . Harding's van, abandoned on a ridge in the middle of nowhere, its tinny radio speaking to no one . . . When Morse and Lewis arrive on the day of the Melbourne Cup, Hereford seems like a ghost town. The tin-roofed shacks and verandahs evoke the Wild West. In many ways 'Promised Land' is a western.

This is made explicit at the climax of the film; the scene opens with a direct reference to *High Noon*. An overhead shot shows Morse standing alone between two railway tracks. He is literally, and metaphorically, on the line. There is nothing arbitrary about this – it has been prepared for. The film is filled with shots featuring strong vertical lines: arcades, road signs, fence posts and gates. And the shots are framed in a way which suggests – in spite of the vastness that surrounds them – that the characters are trapped inside their own little prisons. The Hardings' home seems very small and cramped. There is nothing for Morse to do except go on: 'I let myself be blinded. I have to make amends.' He bravely puts himself in jeopardy to rescue Harding's kidnapped daughter. The tension is released in an explosion of bullets. Morse survives, but he is left with blood all over him.

Opposite *'High Noon' Down Under: Anne Harding makes a mad dash for her daughter.*

One for the album: a colourful culture clash in 'Promised Land'.

However, in some ways, the most remarkable point of the film comes before the shoot-out when, in a highly popular, prime-time programme, the two leading characters talk about *God*. 'What do you think about God and that?' asks Lewis. 'I think there are times when I wish to God there was one,' replies Morse. 'A just god. A god dispensing justice. I'd like to believe in that.' It is a touching, important moment. No other cop-show would have attempted such a scene nor succeeded in getting away with it.

'Promised Land' is a doom-laden episode but there are plenty of lighter moments. Harding the supergrass runs a mower-repair shop. Morse's initial reactions to the new country are delightful and there is something genuinely mind-boggling about seeing him venture into a sheep-shearing shed to the sound of banjos and fiddles. Barrington Pheloung's country and western score is hilarious. The ending, too, is superb.

Back in Sydney, Morse is finally going to see *Der Rosenkavalier* at the Opera House before returning to England the following day. Lewis is going to stay on for a holiday; his wife is flying out to join him. Morse, chastened and lonely, says, 'It's an hour till the matinée, what are you going to do?' Too excited to realise that his boss is asking for company, Lewis announces that he is going to take a trip around the harbour. Morse is left by himself – the sun-drenched steps behind him a dazzling bank of black and white lines – and, as the camera pulls back and as Strauss soars on the soundtrack, the viewer is left with a whopping great lump in the throat.

God, Lewis, what's going on?
'MASONIC MYSTERIES'

Medallion men: Morse, of course, hasn't got one. Colin Dexter is below him.

'MASONIC MYSTERIES', the final episode of the fourth series, was originally broadcast on 24 January 1990. Written by Julian Mitchell and directed by Danny Boyle, it is a brilliant collaboration and represents *Inspector Morse* at its most sublime.

The episode hums with invention right from the start. A title sequence of amazing complexity includes everything from which the rest of the film develops. Even before the words 'Masonic Mysteries' have appeared on the screen, we are plunged into the fantastical world of Mozart's *The Magic Flute*, unwittingly shown the killer and told that during this performance the spotlight is going to be very much on the Inspector himself. As Morse says later, 'It's quite interesting being the hunted for once instead of the hunter.'

Arresting thoughts:
Morse in one of his own
cells in 'Masonic
Mysteries'.

Morse and his latest lady-friend, Beryl Newsome, are attending the final dress rehearsal of an amateur production of Mozart's Masonic opera. The killer, Hugo De Vries, posing as the dresser, sends Morse backstage to fetch his regalia. At the same time Beryl is called to the telephone and stabbed to death, her blood-curdling scream merging with a diva's top note. Morse, who was seen to have upset Beryl earlier on, falls under suspicion. This is only the beginning of a gruelling ordeal. Like the hero of the opera, Morse, in order to survive, must pass various tests along the way. The audience and their hero are in for a hair-raising ride.

Although De Vries is initially thought to be dead, it transpires that he is responsible for everything that has happened to Morse: the campaign of vandalism, computer hacking, theft and murder, all designed to make the man who put him in prison suffer as much as De Vries himself has done. An extremely clever conman and a master of disguise, De Vries, in addition to being the dresser, appears at different points throughout the episode as a tramp to whom Morse gives money, a reader of the *Financial Times*, a press photographer, a journalist who asks Chief Superintendent Strange, 'Any statement yet, sir?' and a by-stander in a park. The action is interspersed with black and white photographs of Morse that turn out to have been taken by De Vries as well.

As the psychopath Ian McDiarmid exudes a chilling insouci-

'I am going to kill you. Or am I?': brilliant psychopath Hugo De Vries in 'Masonic Mysteries'.

ance. Mitchell gives him some terrific lines: 'You're sweating, Morse. It is a disagreeable sight'; 'Why do policemen always go round in pairs like low comedians?'; 'I am going to kill you. Or am I?' The viewer is kept guessing till the very end.

The success of Mitchell and Boyle's film lies in the way the style of the episode becomes an integral part of the story. At its simplest, the plot would be 'Morse is framed'. Framing images is the basis of movie-making; film is a rapid sequence of individual frames. 'Masonic Mysteries' is full of frames. Besides De Vries's black and white snaps which he plasters all over his walls, framed photographs – hanging on walls, sitting on desks – pepper the episode. When Morse and Lewis visit Marian Brooke's house Morse removes a photograph from her dressing table. We are warned to keep our eyes open at the beginning of the programme when the dresser complains, 'You people, you never look.'

People are forever looking out of window frames. The very first shot is of Papageno, dressed as a bird, looking down from a window of the concert hall. He has a bird's-eye view. Seconds later we see the dresser looking out of another window in the same building. When Strange listens to Inspector Bottomley burbling on he looks out of his window. Morse, showing Lewis the Masonic symbols on the tarpaulin covering his car, becomes aware that a neighbour is watching from an upstairs window. When they visit the offices of Amnox someone watches them approach from a first-floor window. As the number of overhead shots suggests, Morse is under surveillance.

This is Hitchcock territory and Boyle acknowledges the fact with references to several of his movies. Two examples will suffice. The long opening shot, seemingly one take, recalls a famous one in *Frenzy* that tracks all the way from Barry Foster's flat, down the stairs, out of the front door and across to the other side of Henrietta Street in Covent Garden. The dizzying overhead shot of Lewis climbing the stairs to Morse's bathroom where he will find the body of Macnutt – 'I don't know why he has a house this size, he never has anyone to stay' – echoes a similar one in *Psycho*. But Boyle is an excellent director in his own terms as well. He knows when to move the camera and when to keep it still. He knows how to use sound and when to have none at all.

When Bottomley finds Morse's beer, crossword, underwear and photograph in Beryl's flat, Morse realises that he is in serious trouble. 'Someone, I don't know who, is trying to frame me.' There is nothing for Bottomley to do except arrest him. Boyle keeps the camera closing in on John Thaw's face – we hear Strange and Bottomley talking but we do not cut to see them – so that our sense of Morse's entrapment is increased. It makes sense to capture every second of such a powerful performance.

A similar approach is used after Morse has been breathalysed by Butterworth on the motorway bridge. Mitchell is good at putting Morse – and therefore Thaw – under pressure. It is a desolate location and a rainy, windy night. While Lewis says goodbye to the motorcycle cop, the camera remains on Morse, alone, sitting behind the wheel of the Jag. There is no music, just the sound of the motorway traffic, the headlights of which can be seen, out of focus through the car window, snaking past. Morse, shoulders slumped, seems dazed. It is a wonderful, forlorn image and one that will be echoed in the very last frame of the film.

But later, when the fire-bomb ignites in Morse's home, the only sound to be heard as the room becomes a raging inferno is

Mozart. We don't hear the crackle of the flames, the voice of the policeman on guard duty or any background noise at all until the glass in the front door is smashed, letting out an explosion of sound. This serves to make the rescue all the more dramatic.

And there is even better to come during the climax of 'Masonic Mysteries' – which is the single most impressive scene out of all the films of *Inspector Morse* so far. Morse has tracked De Vries down to 4 Chippenham Close. They are alone in the front room, surrounded by the photographs taken throughout the episode and symbols from *The Magic Flute*. Lewis has just rung the doorbell. De Vries, gun in hand, orders Morse to stand with his back to him. 'Life and death. Darkness and light. None of it matters.' On the soundtrack, the opera finishes. 'Good-bye.' We see Morse's face in close-up. The tape stops. Silence. Black and white photograph of Morse. Black and white photograph of Beryl. We hear the click of the trigger being pulled. Morse closes his eyes. BANG! The screen goes blank. It stays that way for six seconds.

It was the end of the series. Was it the end of Morse? The viewer breathes a sigh of relief when Morse opens his eyes. Lewis is banging on the front door. De Vries has shot himself. Morse goes to let Lewis in. When they return De Vries has vanished. He has not shot himself. The chase continues.

'Masonic Mysteries' is tremendously exciting, often amusing – the moment when Morse gives Butterworth a Masonic handshake is hilarious – witty and daring. Given the visual expertise, there's a fine irony in the fact that its master-stroke reduces the TV to a mere black square. Such a knowing exploitation of genre can only be done once in a series like *Inspector Morse*. Thanks to such a virtuoso production it could not have been done better.

CHAPTER NINE

THE SECRET
OF SUCCESS

Who said anything about happiness?
'FAT CHANCE'

T HE first screening of 'Masonic Mysteries' was watched by
16.2 million people, more than ever before. In the past ten
years no detective drama has had a higher audience.

A sure sign of the power and influence of *Inspector Morse* came
after the screening of 'Greeks Bearing Gifts' on 20 March 1991. The
climax of this latter-day Greek tragedy, in which a baby appears
to be held over a banister, high above a marble floor – 'They're so
fragile. How do so many of them survive?' – was so convincing
that Lord Jenkins of Hillhead was moved to express concern in
Parliament about the treatment of young children in television.
The child in question was never out of the sight of its mother nor
more than three feet off the floor.

'This sounds terribly irresponsible,' says producer David
Lascelles, 'but I found the whole thing hard to take seriously. I
knew what had happened and, you know, it's called *camera angles*.
A platform was constructed on the other side of the banister. It
seemed so obvious that I was amazed that people should be upset
by it. The tragedy of it was that the episode went out on the same
evening that Eric Clapton's son fell to his death in New York. I'm
sure there was some subconscious link between the two incidents.
Small children and heights are no laughing matter.'

There was no doubt that viewers were taking *Inspector Morse*
seriously. The audience for 'The Dead of Jericho' on 6 January 1987
was 13.9 million. 'Second Time Around', which went out on
20 February 1991, was watched by 15.6 million people.

'When a series reaches this longevity,' says Ted Childs, 'everyone involved worries that it might go off the boil. In my experience,
the problem with successful series is that there's a temptation to
pander to popular demand, to reinforce your appeal. But that way
cliché lies. It's a struggle to continue being original.'

The fact that *Inspector Morse* is a collection of self-contained
films rather than a chain of episodes has guarded against this. Its
ability to change has been important too. Different producers have
different ideas, just as each writer views Morse in their own way.
For the third series Chris Burt took Morse away from the colleges of
Oxford into the city and the countryside that surrounds it. Whereas

Opposite *Chamber of
horrors: Randal Rees looks
down on his dead wife in
'Greeks Bearing Gifts'.*

Chemical reactions: Dr Russell spells it out for the dynamic duo in 'The Secret of Bay 5B'.

'Ghost in the Machine' takes place in and around a magnificent stately home, 'The Secret of Bay 5B' lies in a multi-storey car park. 'I thought there were times when Morse was too pompous,' says Burt. 'I tried to use Lewis and a sense of humour to prick the bubble.' He replaced Max the surly pathologist with sultry Dr Grayling Russell. Morse's uneasy courtship of her was the source of much delight but it was a limiting factor, a soap opera device, that Lascelles, who took over for the fourth series, removed.

'Despite Amanda Hillwood's good performance,' says Lascelles, 'the character was too safe. If Morse and Grayling had circled round each other for ever it would have become boring. If they had had a dramatic bust-up there would have been the problem of where to place it in the series. If they, Heaven forbid, had actually got together and Morse had married her it would have been necessary to kill her off. There was no point to it. If Morse had continued to find other women attractive it would have made him seem like an ageing flirt.'

The sixth series has been produced by Deirdre Keir, who has been responsible for such programmes as *Coming Through*, starring Helen Mirren and Kenneth Branagh, *The Widowmaker* (which was directed by *Morse* man John Madden) and *The One Game*, with Stephen Dillon and Patrick Malahide (who appears in 'Driven to Distraction'). *The One Game* was written by John Brown. Keir, continuing the tradition of bringing in a new writer every year, invited

Opposite Studied expressions: Georgina and Michelle discover a theft in Lord Hanbury's study.

him to contribute a script to her first series of *Inspector Morse*. The result is 'Absolute Conviction', directed by Antonia Bird and starring Diana Quick, Suzanna Hamilton, Jim Broadbent, Richard Wilson and Sean Bean. Eton College chapel stands in for Oxford. It was the first time that a film crew had been granted access to the chapel. Those in charge are fans of *Inspector Morse*.

'I used to talk to Kenny McBain while he was producing the series,' says Keir. 'I have always loved it. When Ted Childs asked me if I'd like to produce *Inspector Morse* I nearly bit his hand off. You have to tread a very, very careful path. You can't just follow a formula and offer more of the same because familiarity breeds contempt. Equally if you don't give the audience what they expect, and continue to provide the elements they like, then they're not going to be happy either. The exciting thing is to explore the programme and see what areas are left after twenty films. Innovation will only satisfy the viewers if they can say, "Yes, that's exactly what Morse and Lewis would do in that situation." You have to bear in mind that the characters are not only policemen but Oxford policemen.'

The other four episodes in the new series are by old hands. Daniel Boyle, who wrote 'Second Time Around', has written two more episodes, 'Dead on Time' and 'Happy Families'. In 'The Last Enemy', which was part of the third series, Morse is asked about his time at university: 'Why did your work go to pieces? A woman?' The answer, of course, is 'yes'. 'Dead on Time' reveals that when he was a student Morse actually became engaged. For some reason he never married. The woman in question went to live in America but in 'Dead on Time' she returns to Oxford because her husband, a Professor of Law, needs treatment for a crippling neurological disease. Morse meets his old flame following the Professor's suicide.

'It is a chamber piece, a love story,' says director John Madden. 'The important thing was to lift it on to a personal plane. It's about Morse rather than anybody else.' 'It's always good to put Morse under pressure,' says Boyle. 'The relationship between Morse and Lewis is very much to the fore.'

In Boyle's second new episode, provisionally called 'Happy Families' and directed by Adrian Shergold, a rich family is being bumped off one by one. Morse, against his wishes, is forced by Superintendent Holdsby to attend a press conference. Two tabloid journalists detect his animosity and start hounding him. They spy on him at home and take secret photographs of him: GENTLEMEN COP and CLEVER DICK scream the headlines. The body count and the pressure continue to mount.

'The Death of the Self' by Alma Cullen, and directed by Colin Gregg, takes Morse to Vicenza and Verona. An old adversary of

Morse, played by Michael Kitchen, surfaces in Italy running a kind of personal-growth outfit. The people who sign on to increase their self-awareness are called Selves. A famous opera singer (played by Frances Barber) is somehow involved in the shady business. Thus the stage is set for some spectacular scenery and the strains of Puccini. Needless to say, Morse does not get on with the local police.

I heard it on the grapevine: Morse investigating the diva.

The series ends, as usual, with an episode by Julian Mitchell. 'Cherubim and Seraphim', directed by Danny Boyle (who is not the same person as writer Daniel Boyle), has a Pied Piper theme. It features an Oxford research don who supplies students with a 'smart' drug that is supposed to improve their mental capacity. 'Think of three things that Morse knows nothing about,' says Mitchell, 'sex, drugs and rock and roll. It is about teenagers and the gulf between them and their parents, how teenagers can go terribly wrong without their parents even realising. Morse doesn't have any children but Lewis has. Morse has a romantic attitude towards children, he feels they're rather wonderful. He remembers his own childhood and applies it to the present case but, of course, it doesn't apply. You learn things about his childhood that have never been revealed before, including the *real* reason he refuses to use his first name. It's very, very sad. A six-Kleenex job.'

Hoping to entice them into the Oxford Playhouse: a billboard in the city rides high on the Morse phenomenon.

As Lewis's mother used to say, 'Laughing always come to crying.' Part of the appeal of *Inspector Morse* certainly lies in its ability to make us laugh and cry – but then so does *The Wizard of Oz*. Nowadays its popularity is largely attributable to John Thaw and Kevin Whately who, thanks to their excellent performances, have both attracted a huge following. Women want to marry or mother them; men envy or identify with them. Quality is in itself attractive. McBain and Childs got what they wanted: a series that was 'well crafted, well written, well acted and well directed.'

There is, of course, an insatiable appetite for detective drama world wide. Each episode of *Morse* provides all the basic ingredients: a corpse or corpses, suspects and clues. The mystery of whodunnit and how they did it certainly creates some – but only some – of the interest. The plot, although complicated, is often conventional. The dénouement, in contrast to the climax of the action, is sometimes banal. It's rather like the long struggle to solve a tricky crossword clue – when you eventually come up with the solution the word itself is frequently commonplace. It is the journey that counts. At least some of the audience must be content to sit back and watch Morse and Lewis unravelling the problem secure in the knowledge that they will get there in the end. Morse would no doubt quote T. S. Eliot who said that the greatest poetry frequently communicates without being understood.

Although *Inspector Morse* is set in the present, it is in fact anything but contemporary. Its durability springs from this timelessness. For a modern detective series there is an astonishing lack of police procedure. Advisers may ensure that the charges brought against a suspect are accurate but there only seem to be three detectives in the city. The programme is far more concerned with pace than with PACE, the Police and Criminal Evidence Act. In the fourth and fifth series there is an attempt to evoke the atmosphere of a bustling Thames Valley cop-shop, and Lewis is seen tapping away on a computer, but how many DCIs drive around in their own vintage car and take naps in the afternoon? There is little violence and less sex. Morse is a sort of Philip Larkin figure, unlucky in love, swanning round the Oxford of the 1950s – where there is never a shortage of parking spaces – dreaming of books and beer. Morse and Lewis are the kind of people we can depend on and trust. In an age when corruption appears to be endemic to all levels of society their innate decency and passionate belief in justice strikes an emotional chord.

In 'Who Killed Harry Field?' Morse says, 'It's always later than you think.' *Inspector Morse* is an elegy, a lament for the misery of human beings and the evil that they do, conducted against the dying of the light. At the end of the day there is something irredeemably indulgent in shutting out the world, switching on the answerphone and curling up, safe in the arms of a sofa, to spend two whole hours wallowing in melancholy. The gliding camerawork and sophisticated use of music are deliberately seductive. The consolations of genre should not be underestimated.

If nostalgia and wish-fulfilment play a part in the appeal, so does *schadenfreude*, pleasure in the misfortunes of others. Over the years, dozens of people have died for our delectation. They have been shot, strangled and stabbed; bludgeoned, poisoned and drowned; pushed from high places, crushed by a car and even crucified. Madness runs in the series. Disease – alcoholism, bulimia, cancer – is everywhere. A succession of neurotic and obnoxious young men cause havoc. Suicide is never far away. Crime springs from disappointment, frustration and despair. It is in the serious treatment of these subjects that *Inspector Morse* transcends its genre. The detective element provides a framework within which each writer can explore universal concerns in their own particular way. In a word, the subject of *Morse* is the same as that of the greatest drama, life. It shows us that in our anger, agony or loneliness we are not alone. Morse has always been aware of this. No wonder then, in 'The Wolvercote Tongue' as in every film, he is morose:

'God, people's lives, Lewis. People's lives . . . and loves.' It is reassuring to know that Morse and Lewis are always there to sort the world out.

WELCOME BACK

They've written about me in the paper, Lewis
'HAPPY FAMILIES'

'DEAD On Time', the first episode of the sixth series, generated a vast number of column inches. Whether the media – and newspapers in particular – helped boost the nation's growing obsession with Inspector Morse or merely reflected it is a moot point but there is no doubt that the audience figures, which had remained steady throughout the sixth series, showed a dramatic increase during the seventh, reaching their peak with the 'final' film, 'Twilight Of The Gods' on 20 January 1993, which attracted 18.8 million viewers. It was the fifth most watched individual programme of the year and to date is still the highest performing drama on UK television since 1990.

No other television series has captured the public's imagination in the same way. The nearest thing to Morse mania since then has centred on Victor Meldrew, the miserable old git brilliantly played by Richard Wilson (Brian Thornton in 'Absolute Conviction') in the BBC situation comedy *One Foot In The Grave*. His flamboyant whinging struck a chord in a country undergoing its own crisis of confidence. As regards detective drama, Granada's *Cracker* has been the only serious contender. Its strengths are Jimmy McGovern's scripts and Robbie Coltrane's excellent performance in the title role but the series is hampered by the single-hour format. In addition the relentless in-your-face style and taste for sensationalism occasionally become wearisome.

'Dead On Time' got the tabloids fizzing because it reunites Morse with his long-lost love, Susan Fallon (Joanna David, whom Thaw once directed in David Halliwell's *Little Malcolm And His Struggle Against The Eunuchs*), only to have him lose her again. It is devastating drama, certainly one of the best episodes ever, but the great virtue of Daniel Boyle's screenplay is the way it develops the relationship of Morse and Lewis. Heart-broken by the suicide of Susan, the Chief Inspector is unable to comprehend that she could have killed her husband (albeit out of kindness). Lewis once again has to protect his boss by destroying the evidence (a tape from a telephone answering machine). This final scene is actually more moving than Susan's death because the viewer has known both the characters for years. 'D'you feel like breakfast?' asks Morse. 'Will you be paying?' replies Lewis, hopefully. 'I don't seem to have any money.' 'So it's down to me then.' 'Let's just say it's one I owe you.' 'Yeah. Let's just say that.' Morse will never know just how much he owes Lewis. This is dramatic irony at its best.

Opposite *The agony and the ecstasy: Lewis, in party hat, and Morse behold the brave new world of youth culture in 'Cherubim And Seraphim'*

The morning after the night before: Lewis looks after Morse in 'Dead On Time'.

Opposite *Shooting a policeman: penman Billy (Rupert Graves, left) and lensman Chas (Jamie Foreman) in 'Happy Families'.*

But it is not all doom and gloom. Mr William Bryce-Morgan with his mechanical bucking bronco – 'it doesn't eat, it doesn't pooh!' – and one-eyed Scottish butler, McGregor, are a hilarious double act. And hints of Lewis's home-life provide further amusement: 'I'm a steak and baked spud man myself but Mrs Lewis likes to live on the culinary edge, as it were.' They are only off to an Indian restaurant.

Boyle's pawky humour also enlivens 'Happy Families'. Told that Chief Superintendent Strange is on holiday in Bangkok, Morse asks Lewis 'What's a man of his age doing in a place like that?' The fact that the innocent Morse has no idea makes it doubly funny. An Agatha Christie-like tale of *nouveaux riches* being haunted and hunted by old secrets, 'Happy Families' has a refreshing irreverence. Part One ends with the tabloid hack who hounds Morse (wittily played by a goatee-bearded Rupert Graves) flicking a V-sign at the camera and Colin Dexter, seen at the champagne reception in 'Dead On Time', swaps his dinner-jacket for the rags of a drunken tramp whom we see brawling in Carfax. It is as if nobody is taking the mystery element of the plot – which descends into pure flapdoodle at the close – too seriously. Lewis dons cowboy gear for the police fair where Morse sheepishly wins a pink elephant. And when Morse's Jaguar fails to start first time outside Hertford College at the end of Part Two and Thaw turns to look at Whately you can sense the smiles between them.

But on-screen things are not so friendly between Morse and Lewis. Harassed by the press and unable to crack the case, Morse vents his frustration on Lewis: 'Don't you tell me how to behave. Don't.' The publicity-conscious Superintendent Holdsby takes Morse off the case – the first time such a thing has happened to him in his twenty-year career – but eventually, as the police fête has it,

*Cuddly toy: Morse
and friend in 'Happy
families'*

the 'clever dick' of the headlines finds the identity of the murderer
at the bookstall.

If it seems that the overworked policemen need a holiday,
'The Death Of The Self' provides one. Indeed this Italian job turns
out not to involve murder at all, just the smuggling of works of art.
Writer Alma Cullen neatly reverses the premise of 'Promised Land'
so that this time round Morse is delighted to be abroad whereas
Lewis, who cannot speak the lingo and does not like the food, is
anxious to return home so that he can take part in the fathers' race
at his son's sports day. Director Colin Gregg makes the most of
the glorious locations. The early scene in which the camera pulls
back from a white sky to reveal Nicola Burgess practising scales
on the terrace of her Palladian villa never ceases to cause goose-
bumps.

Antonia Bird's 'Absolute Conviction' brings Morse back to earth
with a bump – literally. John Brown's story of argy-bargy in an open
prison takes an almost cruel pleasure in humiliating the middle-

Behind bars: Morse left high and dry in the prison gym of 'Absolute Conviction'.

aged man. Morse nearly crashes his Jaguar while looking at a picture of the governor Hilary Stephens (Diana Quick); he falls over in the Covered Market while chasing Charlie Bennett (Jim Broadbent); and cuts a very sorry figure as he interviews the fitness fan Roland Sherman and the footballing Alex Bailey (Sean Bean), the latter leaving him looking helpless in front of the empty goal in the deserted sports hall. The coarser language and Bird's habit of having extras forever walking in between the leading characters and the camera brought a busy, ballsy realism to the series, signalled at the very start of the film when the shot of an idyllic desert island is revealed to be just a travel agent's poster.

'Cherubim And Seraphim' begins as 'Absolute Conviction' ends: with grey skies and rain. It is a sombre episode in which the theme of culture clash, of the shock of the new, is mirrored in the way that Danny Boyle directs it. The opening shot of a young raver being raked by lasers serves notice that we are entering a grave new world.

The light fantastic:
The balcony scene
from 'Cherubim And
Seraphim'

When Superintendent Strange admits 'I can't imagine you young Morse' he is speaking for all of us – but as Morse investigates the suicide of his step-niece he gradually reveals his own unhappy childhood. 'No one can imagine someone else's pain, Robbie. It's the human tragedy.' For all the new drugs and new music of the New Age, the problems of growing up and growing old remain the same. 'Is there something wrong with the beer, sir?' asks the publican in Part Four (played by writer Julian Mitchell himself). 'No, no, it's me.

Something wrong with me,' replies Morse. Everybody has their own little vice, takes their consolation where they can. Morse may never have used drugs but he usually drowns his sorrows in alcohol; Mrs Lewis is involved with Cyprus Sherry Week; and Strange nibbles – guiltily – his chocolate digestives.

If there are times during the sixth series when the mellow drama of Inspector Morse modulates into sheer melodrama the seventh returns to the golden days of classic conundrums for the first two films but finishes with a magnificent flourish which seems to ask, just how far can Inspector Morse go?

In 'Deadly Slumber', a tale of murder and malpractice centring on the Brewster Clinic, director Stuart Orme (whose previous credits include the ground-breaking but underrated thriller series *The Fear* and the film *The Wolves of Willoughby Chase*) uses a variety of crane shots to great picturesque effect. And yet, in some ways, the most moving moment comes when Morse is told that the life support machine keeping Michael Stepping's daughter Avril alive has been turned off. Until that point the camera has viewed the characters, who are trapped in grief, from behind bars – the railings of a banister, vertical blinds – but now it goes out through the open window of the hospital room for the very first time. It is time to let go; Avril has been granted a merciful release.

Psychopath John Peter Barrie engineers his own release in 'The Day Of The Devil'. Like Hugo De Vries in 'Masonic Mysteries' before him, Barrie is a master of disguise and shadows Morse and Lewis as they enter a Grand Guignol world of satanic worship. Although the jargon-spouting Sergeant Brenner of the Tactical Support Group provides some light relief – as does Lewis's astonishing remark, 'exegeses on ancient grimoires' – the result is a spectacular but grim story of the devastating effects of rape, a case which

Calm on the surface: idyllic shots like this can sometimes only be achieved by going to great lengths. One crane sequence in 'Deadly Slumber' required a track to be laid on a platform above the water.

'An exegesis on ancient grimoires?': Humphrey Appleton (Richard Griffiths) discusses satanic chapter and verse in 'The Day Of The Devil'.

shatters Morse's belief in what he sees as the 'cuddly' qualities of women.

'Twilight Of The Gods' destroys another of Morse's romantic illusions: that artists in general, and prima donnas in particular, are superior beings. Gwladys Probert (Sheila Gish) may be, in Morse's words, 'the greatest diva of her time' but 'the Welsh canary bird' also turns out to be a foul-mouthed nymphomaniac who thinks nothing of using her younger sister as bait for the boyos. As usual it is Lewis's homespun wisdom that provides the antidote: 'My dad used to love football but he didn't like footballers. You have to keep the people who do things apart from what they do.' Media mogul Andrew Baydon (Robert Hardy), who has seen rather more of life and death, berates Morse for his innocence: 'You're so English. You've led such a sheltered English life.'

Julian Mitchell's version of Götterdämmerung begins in glorious sunshine and, in a stroke of genius, has Morse on top of the world – a very peculiar sight. But the tone gradually and steadily darkens. The concentrated camp of the operatic circus (exemplified by Probert's flouncing and flirting entourage) gives way to the sheer horror of the concentration camps, summarized with characteristic

brutality by Baydon as 'life or death every minute of the day. My life or yours. Can you understand that, knobhead?'

In many ways 'Twilight Of The Gods', which was thought to be Morse's last outing on television, pastiches all the episodes that come before it. The dreamy detective spends most of the time investigating the wrong case and has to be set on the right track by Lewis. The familiar photogenic locations of Oxford are exploited to the full by director Herbie Wise (who also directed 'Ghost In The Machine'); and both Town (a flippant florist, a snobbish dog-walker, a dead journalist) and Gown (the procession to the Sheldonian and the Encaenia Tea) play their part. Morse's last case involves the crime of the century, genocide. His faith in art and humanity has been shaken. It ends, as it should, with him driving home – alone – through the dusk.

The star-studded cast is assisted by several notable cameos. Charles Walker-Wise, the director's son, plays Lord Hinksey's page boy; writer Julian Mitchell plays the doctor who tells a nurse in Part Three to 'check the gasses every quarter of an hour please'; and last and least yours truly plays the rapt concert-goer sitting on Morse's right in the Holywell Music Room during the title sequence.

Broad humour: Lord Hinksey (Sir John Gielgud) on his way to the Sheldonian Theatre in 'Twilight Of The Gods'. Director Herbert Wise's son, Charles Walker-Wise, is the page-boy.

Spot the dummy: my moment of glory, sitting on Morse's right in the Holywell Music Room in the opening sequence of 'Twilight Of The Gods'. Dr Robert Gasser, who can be glimpsed in many an episode, is on Morse's left. Bursar of Brasenose College, he liaises between the producers of the series and the University of Oxford, helping the film-makers find the best locations. The woman sitting behind him is Susan McCulloch, the opera singer who provided the vocals for actress Sheila Gish to mime.

Every dog has his day and mine – Wednesday 19 August 1992 – began at 6.30 a.m. After breakfast (a bacon butty and mug of tea) at the deserted coalyard serving as unit base, myself and the hundred or so other extras were ferried to the location by coach so that we were on set by 8.30 a.m. The crew, needless to say, took the mickey out of me at every opportunity. As wardrobe master Tony Allen straightened my tie and make-up man Robin Grantham powdered my shiny nose, John Thaw looked on with amusement. 'Aren't we in danger of overgilding the lily?' he asked. 'Naah,' came the reply. 'You can't polish crap.' I got my own back after lunch when I told Mr Thaw that one of the extras had asked me if I was playing Morse's nephew. 'I don't look that old,' he said, somewhat crestfallen.

It was 4.00 p.m. before our section of the audience finally came in front of the camera. As it glided along its tracks towards us butterflies flew up from nowhere in my stomach and my face felt as though a million baby snakes were writhing beneath the skin. The second time was easier, the third better still, but it is difficult laughing at a joke that you have been hearing all day. I now appreciate that patience and perseverance are just as important as the performance. By 6.00 p.m. I was exhausted and exhilarated. And it's true what they say about television making you look fat.

Opposite Keeping it close to his chest: Morse contemplates 'Welsh canary-bird' Gwladys Probert in 'Twilight Of The Gods'.

* * *

Taking five: a quiet moment during a break in filming 'Twilight Of The Gods'.

A [man] can have enough of his own four walls
– 'THE WAY THROUGH THE WOODS'

Early June 1995. The fifth and final week of principal photography on 'The Way Through The Woods', the twenty-ninth film featuring Chief Inspector Morse. It is a typical English summer's day: breezy, chilly and damp. Every so often the sun manages to break through the low grey cloud but only fitfully - as if God were testing his arc-lights.

The shabby Territorial Army centre in Harrow, north London, is once again doubling as a cop-shop in the Thames valley. It is several years since the cast and crew were cluttering up its corridors: the derelict Ministry of Defence laboratory in Harefield, used in later series, has now disappeared beneath a housing development whose roads are named after those involved with Inspector Morse. Further proof, if any were needed, of the lasting effect that the series has had on the viewing public.

'People never stopped asking me when Inspector Morse was coming back,' says John Thaw relaxing in the trailer which he shares with Kevin Whately. 'Even now, when I go into the supermarket, folk come up to me and say that they miss it and when I tell them that we're doing one at the moment their little faces light up.'

Since 'Twilight Of The Gods' went out Thaw has been seen taking French leave in *A Year In Provence*, trying to win an election for the Labour Party in David Hare's *The Absence Of War* at the Royal National Theatre (which was also filmed for Screen Two) and wearing a horsehair wig in *Kavanagh QC*. What prompted him to return to the role of the depressive detective?

'Well, for a start, Ted Childs kept on about it and the thought of doing just one film – one based on Colin Dexter's *The Way Through*

Cast and crew:
Kevin and continuity
supervisor Pauline
Harlow.

The Woods which I had read and enjoyed – was much more attractive than doing a whole series. To cut a long story short a friend said to me, 'It's five weeks out of your life and you will give a lot of pleasure to a lot of people. What are you going to do if you don't do it? Sit at home and watch the grass grow?' Actually I love doing that but, looked at in that way, I thought why not? So here we are.'

Kevin Whately returns from lunch and changes into the right suit for the next scene. 'Both Kevin and I were worried that we might not be able to recreate the relationship between Morse and Lewis,' says Thaw. 'I haven't seen any of the rushes but I think we have.' 'Yes,' says Whately. 'It was a bit like putting on an old coat and finding that it fits you. I think the special chemistry is still there.' 'We were both pretty nervous on the first day,' continues Thaw, 'but ultimately it was like getting on a bike – you never forget how to ride one.'

Have they changed over the past three years? Do they feel the same way about their characters? 'I certainly feel older,' says Thaw ruefully, 'and I must have changed because I've done other things since. Every acting experience, no matter how small, adds to you in some way. I still feel the same about Morse though. I like some of his qualities but not others – for instance he can be a pompous old sod at times. But it's not up to me, John Thaw, to judge him. If the scene requires him to be a supercilious so-and-so then that's what I play. It's my job. Of course, that's when journalists saying oh, John Thaw gives us his miserable old swine again.' He laughs. 'They forget it's not really me.'

'My feelings about Lewis haven't changed either,' says Whately. 'My main problem with him is his hair style. They said I could change it this time round but I thought it better to stick with the

*Bloodied but unbowed:
Lewis hits the right
track in 'The Way
Through The Woods'.*

toupee effect' – he pats the flat mat of hair on his head – 'but, to be honest with you, I hate it.'

On the evidence of Russell Lewis's script, 'The Way Through The Woods' promises to be a hair-raising experience. It concerns the disappearance of a young female hitch-hiker. Morse, as usual, cannot see the wood for the trees which brings him into conflict not only with another DCI (played by Malcolm Storry) but also with Lewis. The explosive climax in Wytham Woods (last seen in 'The Mystery Of Bay 5B') rivals that of 'Promised Land'.

'Although Russell Lewis has not written a Morse script before I think he's done a very good job,' says Thaw. 'He's reintroduced many of the familiar ingredients of the series and come up with a virtual condensation of it. There's less romance than usual but, let's put it this way, if we had been doing a three-hour film rather than a two-hour film there is a woman whom Morse would no doubt have attempted to seduce.'

Morse meets Claire Osborne (Vivienne Ritchie) at a concert at Lonsdale College. Eagle-eyed viewers should be able to spot Colin Dexter among the throng. He appears in the same shot as his (and my) long-suffering editor, Maria Rejt.

'There are some big scenes between Morse and Lewis,' says Whately. 'Lewis's patience is finally beginning to give out. He needs to prove to himself that he can be a detective without Morse looking over his shoulder all the time.' 'I think it's the first time that Lewis says that he's had enough and that he's going,' says Thaw. 'It's a blow, to say the least.'

Inspector Morse came to an end, albeit temporarily, because as actors Thaw and Whately had had enough. 'It was like being on a treadmill,' says Thaw. 'I said to Kevin this morning, "We're coming to the end of a shoot, how would you feel if you knew you had another film to shoot next week?"' They both pull long faces. 'I decided to leave *Peak Practice* for the same reason,' says Whately. 'I'm always amazed when something I'm in is successful but after three series I feel that I've done as much as I can in the role. I would like to concentrate on single films now. For example the next project I hope to take part in is former Morse writer Anthony Minghella's screen version of Michael Ondaatje's novel *The English Patient*.'

John Thaw has agreed to don his wig once again for a second series of *Kavanagh QC*. Both he and Whately seem happier and more relaxed in their work than they were three years ago. 'It has been like old times but with less pressure,' says Whately. 'Morse was never supposed to be a prison sentence,' says Thaw. 'I think we have both enjoyed ourselves this time round.' Does this mean that we have not yet seen the last of the unparalleled pair? They smile. 'Let's assume', says Thaw, 'that, like Tonto and the Lone Ranger, they'll go on to a new adventure. There is a possibility, no, a probability that we will make another film next year. Probably based on another of Colin's books.'

'The Daughters Of Cain' would be the thirtieth episode of Inspector Morse. A magnificent achievement. Keep your fingers crossed.

SERIES ONE
Producer Kenny McBain

'The Dead of Jericho'
(directed by Alastair Reid, written by Anthony Minghella)
6 January 1987

'The Silent World of Nicholas Quinn'
(directed by Brian Parker, written by Julian Mitchell)
13 January 1987

'Service of all the Dead'
(directed by Peter Hammond, written by Julian Mitchell)
20 January 1987

Grim reflections: Morse in 'Service of all the Dead'.

Opposite Fall from grace: Jan Harvey as ex-TV presenter Friday Rees – 'the face that launched a thousand clips' – in 'Greeks Bearing Gifts'.

Guided tour: Dr Kemp leads Morse through the Ashmolean Museum to see the Wolvercote Buckle.

SERIES TWO
PRODUCER KENNY MCBAIN

'The Wolvercote Tongue'
(directed by Alastair Reid, written by Julian Mitchell)
25 December 1987

'Last Seen Wearing'
(directed by Edward Bennett, written by Thomas Ellice)
8 March 1988

'The Settling of the Sun'
(directed by Peter Hammond, written by Charles Wood)
15 March 1988

'Last Bus to Woodstock'
(directed by Peter Duffell, written by Michael Wilcox)
22 March 1988

SERIES THREE
PRODUCER CHRIS BURT

'Ghost in the Machine'
(directed by Herbert Wise, written by Julian Mitchell)
4 January 1989

'The Last Enemy'
(directed by James Scott, written by Peter Buckman)
11 January 1989

'Deceived by Flight'
(directed by Anthony Simmons, written by Anthony Minghella)
18 January 1989

'The Secret of Bay 5B'
(directed by Jim Goddard, written by Alma Cullen)
25 January 1989

Still life: Morse and Professor Reece in 'The Last Enemy'. The latter will soon drink his last.

Sergeants at arms:
Sergeant Maitland listens
to Sergeant Lewis in
'Driven to Distraction'.

SERIES FOUR
PRODUCER DAVID LASCELLES

'The Infernal Serpent'
(directed by John Madden, written by Alma Cullen)
3 January 1990

'The Sins of the Fathers'
(directed by Peter Hammond, written by Jeremy Burnham)
10 January 1990

'Driven to Distraction'
(directed by Sandy Johnson, written by Anthony Minghella)
17 January 1990

'Masonic Mysteries'
(directed by Danny Boyle, written by Julian Mitchell)
24 January 1990

SERIES FIVE
PRODUCER DAVID LASCELLES

'Second Time Around'
(directed by Adrian Shergold, written by Daniel Boyle)
20 February 1991

'Fat Chance'
(directed by Roy Battersby, written by Alma Cullen)
27 February 1991

'Who Killed Harry Field?'
(directed by Colin Gregg, written by Geoffrey Case)
13 March 1991

'Greeks Bearing Gifts'
(directed by Adrian Shergold, written by Peter Nichols)
20 March 1991

'Promised Land'
(directed by John Madden, written by Julian Mitchell)
27 March 1991

'Is this a dagger which I see before me?': Dinah Newbury confronts the Managing Director of Think Thin in 'Fat Chance'.

Keeping his hair on: Preparing for the next scene in 'The Death of the Self'

SERIES SIX
PRODUCER DEIRDRE KEIR

'Dead On Time'
(Directed by John Madden, written by Daniel Boyle)
26 February 1992

'Happy Families'
(Directed by Adrian Shergold, written by Daniel Boyle)
11 March 1992

'The Death of the Self'
(Directed by Colin Gregg, written by Alma Cullen)
25 March 1992

'Absolute Conviction'
(Directed by Antonia Bird, written by John Brown)
8 April 1992

'Cherubim And Seraphim'
(Directed by Danny Boyle, written by Julian Mitchell)
15 April 1992

SERIES SEVEN
PRODUCER CHRIS BURT

'Deadly Slumber'
(Directed by Stuart Orme, written by Daniel Boyle)
6 January 1993

'The Day Of The Devil'
(Directed by Stephen Whittaker, written by Daniel Boyle)
13 January 1993

'Twilight Of The Gods'
(Directed by Herbert Wise, written by Julian Mitchell)
20 January 1993

SERIES EIGHT
PRODUCER CHRIS BURT

'The Way Through The Woods'
(Directed by John Madden, written by Russell Lewis)

I WOULD like to thank the following people: Colin Dexter, John Thaw and Kevin Whately; Ted Childs, Angela Elkins, Barry Ledingham, Nick Lockett, Peter Lucas, Tracy Munro, Pat Truman de Reimers, Deborah Waight and Tim Whitby of Central Independent Television; Deirdre Keir (producer Series VI); Chris Burt (producer Series III, VII and 'The Way Through The Woods'); Fliss Coombs at Zenith for assistance way beyond the call of duty and every else at Zenith for their help; my editors, Maria Rejt and Claire Evans of Macmillan, for their patience; Peter Ward, for designing the book; the management of *Time Out* magazine; Howard Moore for his invaluable word-processing skills, TSMS Services Ltd for statistical research; and everybody who granted me interviews even though, for them, it was often a difficult and inconvenient time. Without the encouragement and support of them all this book would not have been possible.

M.S.

The publishers would like to credit the following photographers for the photographs appearing on the jacket and inside the book:

Tony Nutley (front and back cover) Richard Blanshard, John Brown, David Farrell, Tom Hilton, Peter Kernot, Daniel Meadows, Simon Mein, Stephen Morley, Ian Pleeth, Sarah Quill, Tony Russell, Mike Vaughan.

The publishers would like to thank all those people who appear in the photographs and who have granted their permission for us to reproduce their photographs in this book:

Frances Barber, Irina Brook, Maurice Bush, Simon Callow, members of the Cookham Cantorium, Kenneth Colley, Brian Cox, Rainbow Dench, Maurice Denham, Rhondda Findleton, Jamie Foreman, Barry Foster, Sir John Gielgud, Rupert Graves, Richard Griffiths, James D. Grout, Kenneth Haigh, Jan Harvey, Amanda Hillwood, Patricia Hodge, John Jarratt, Martin Jarvis, Karl Jenkinson, Alex Jennings, Freddie Jones, Gemma Jones, James Laurenson, Ian McDiarmid, Patrick Malahide, Fiona Mollison, Angela Morant, John Normington, Mary Jo Randle, Norman Rodway, David Ryall, Caroline Ryder, Roberta Taylor, Kim Thomson, Charlie Walker-Wise, Zoë Wanamaker, Peter Woodthorpe and Barrington Pheloung (original music composer).

Members of the Zenith crews: Tony Breeze (Focus Puller), Lucy Bristow (Clapper Loader), Chris Burt (Producer), Michael Davis (Director of Photography), Tim Dodd (Focus Puller), Karen Ferguson (Hairdresser), Robin Grantham (Make-up), Colin Gregg (Director), Bill Kirk (First Assistant Director), Lou Lavelly (Camera Operator), Dickie Lee (Grip), James Scott (Director), Bob Shipsey (Clapper Loader), Nigel Slatter (Camera Operator), Richard Styles (Third Assistant Director).

Our thanks are also due to Colin Dexter and Julian Mitchell for their kindness in sending in material for the book and to Roger Hancock Ltd for permission to reproduce the photograph of the late Kenny McBain.

While every effort has been made to trace artists featured photographically in this book, the publishers will be glad to make proper acknowledgement in future editions of this publication in the event that any unavoidable omissions have occurred by the time of going to press.